THE GUID

MW00364372

Sᴇx

Member Handbook

1st Edition

MEMBER NAME: _____

TITLE: _____
(choose member title from below)

DATE: _____

SIGNATURE: _____

The Guide to Laughing (GTL) Institute welcomes the owner of this book (whose name appears above), as a member of the GTL Institute and entitles them to all member privileges including, but not limited to:

- Helping others to laugh and learn about life.
- Rejuvenating the mind, body, and spirit of oneself and others with shared laughter.
- Contributing "insightful observations" to future Guide to Laughing handbooks.
- Inviting new members into the Guide to Laughing Institute.

Your only obligations as a GTL Institute member are to **enjoy life** and **share laughter** (see page 8).

Member titles

Apostle of Humility	Goddess	Urban Shaman
Emissary of Optimism	Healing Minister	Spiritual Counselor
Flying Missionary	Mirth Messenger	Prof. of Absolute Reality

THE GUIDE TO LAUGHING AT SEX
MEMBER HANDBOOK
1ST EDITION

Executive Editor · Shawn Gold
Editor · Kiersten Burke
Assistant Editor · Bianca Harzbecker
Assistant Editor · Holly Schwarz

Book Design · Digital Soup
Brand Strategy · Tom Ackerman & Davia Smith
Illustration · Don Anderson
Conceptual Design · Randy Horton
Producer · Margie Gilmore
Spaghetti Wall · Marc Shaiman & Scott Wittman

Library of Congress Control Number: 2003109742
ISBN 0-972963-61-8
Typeset in House Industries Chalet™ and Sign Painter™ families
Printed in Canada

Distributed in North America by CDS Books
425 Madison Avenue
New York, 10017

Published by Handy Logic Press
8033 Sunset Blvd, #490
Los Angeles, CA 90046

10 9 8 7 6 5 4 3 2 1

The "insightful observations" in this book were gathered enthusiastically but
unscientifically over many years and contributed by hundreds of friends and
acquaintances. Some arrived on cocktail napkins, phone answering machines,
emails and through conversations. Every effort was made to be exact in re-
telling the observations contained herein, but inevitably mistakes were made.
To the original sources and contributors, our sincere gratitude, and where
appropriate, our sincere apologies. Please contact us at Handy Logic Press with
any corrections and we will do our best to make those changes in subsequent
editions.

Table of Contents

3

FOREPLAY

THE SEX ACT

ENJOYING SEX

Step 4: EXPERIMENTING

FANTASY

KINKY SEX

Step 5: COMMON PROBLEMS

Step 6: SEX AND SOCIETY

The Guide To Laughing Institute

The Power of Laughter

Laughter is an innate reaction we have as humans and its potency with regard to our well-being is undeniable. Dating as far back as ancient Greece, hospitals were built next to amphitheatres because the "mirth" of the audience was thought to heal patients. Even the Book of Proverbs in the Old Testament contains verses like "A cheerful heart is as good as medicine, but a downcast spirit dries up the bones."

Laughter is irrefutably contagious and many times more powerful when shared. A funny situation shared among friends is immensely more enjoyable than when experienced alone. The power of laughter's contagion is illustrated everywhere from the collective snickers of children in a classroom to the use of television laugh tracks to elicit laughter from the viewing audience.

In his 1979 autobiography, *Anatomy of an Illness,* Norman Cousins brought the issue of humor therapy to the attention of the medical community. Cases like his, in which laughter therapy brought terminally ill patients to good health, helped popularize the subject. But it wasn't until 1989—when the *Journal of the American Medical Association (JAMA)* acknowledged that laughter helps improve the quality of life for patients with chronic illnesses—that laughter therapy was recognized as a legitimate form of treatment, which brings immediate, symptom-relieving effects. This initiated studies around the world, essentially proving that mirth strengthens, and negative emotions like depression and anger weaken the immune system. Today, the effects of laughter are considered a powerful weapon in the fight against AIDS, cancer, and other diseases.

For even the healthiest people, laughter is needed to maintain wellness both mentally and physically. The stress and strain of conflicts and tension around us can compound our everyday concerns, contributing to a rise in anxiety and depression. For overall wellness, laughter therapy takes on its biggest responsibility: preventing illness by providing a daily release for the body's negative energies and allowing us to focus on the positive.

The Mission

"WELLNESS THROUGH LAUGHTER"

The *Guide to Laughing Institute* recognizes the power of laughter and is doing its part to create a sense of wellness and perspective in the world. Our intention is to help people laugh and learn about life and to connect with each other through shared laughter.

To this end, we continue to collect humorous and "insightful observations" about life from around the world and present them in a fun, concise and sharable format. The *GTL Institute* member handbooks serve as a no-nonsense guide to laughing at life and putting problems in perspective. They are designed as an aid to help people discover the lighter side of life's issues, communicate those findings, and connect with others—and to laugh, snicker, giggle, chuckle, cackle, snort, hoot and guffaw.

> *Let us be grateful to people who make us happy; they are the charming gardeners who make our souls BLOSSOM.*
>
> MARCEL PROUST (1871–1922)
> FRENCH NOVELIST

Insightful Observations

The Guide to Laughing Institute honors those selected to be in this book for their wit and wisdom, for helping others laugh and learn about SEX, and for the impact they have had on our culture.

Their insightful observations have been selected based on the unique perspective they offer, for how concisely they convey wit and wisdom on a given subject, and for their balance of humor, irony, and the unvarnished truth.

Because insightful humor comes in many forms, the observations contained herein are broken out into three primary viewpoints: the **IDEALIST**, the **REALIST**, and the **CYNIC**. Next to each observation, you will see an icon or emoticon that denotes the attitude and perspective of the expert, as it relates to the topic:

 The Idealist: An optimist, one who is predisposed to a positive outcome; the Idealist finds humor in picturesque fantasies and delights in romantic expectations.

 The Realist: One who is inclined to finding a literal truth. They enjoy humor that sheds light on a practical way of approaching or assessing a situation or of solving a problem.

 The Cynic: One who instinctively questions or disagrees with assertions or generally accepted conclusions. A person of wit, who negatively focuses on the incongruities of life and seems to enjoy it.

> *Humor is just another defense against the Universe.*
>
> MEL BROOKS (1926–) WRITER, PRODUCER, DIRECTOR

Member Obligations

ENJOY LIFE

It is more important to have fun than to be funny. Laughter is not so much about jokes as it is about being playful and finding the humor in everyday life. As we mature, life's issues can overwhelm us, causing us to enjoy less and stress more. It is commonly recognized that adults laugh around fifteen times a day, while children laugh *several hundred* times a day. Because laughter in children is so closely associated with play, it is thought that adults laugh less than children simply because they play less. As a *GTL Institute* member, you are charged with opening up to the humor in everyday experiences, recapturing the spirit of play, and celebrating life. By enjoying life, you will become contagious and will have a significant impact on the well-being of those around you.

SHARE LAUGHTER

The *GTL Institute* believes that the essence of life is to connect with people and that the key to connection is laughter. Making a *laughter connection* is one of the best ways to firm up an old friendship or recognize a new one. It is a form of positive social interaction for every culture because it unites people based on the things they enjoy and the way they see life. Anyone can learn to share laughter and help others laugh. It does not mean telling jokes (unless this is one of your talents); it means sharing your humorous perspective and giving others permission to do the same. As you continue to laugh and learn about life, we hope you spread your newfound knowledge to others and join the *GTL Institute* in creating a circle of laughter and mirth.

I Agree _____
(member initials)

Laughter is the shortest distance between two people.

VICTOR BORGE (1909–2000) CLOWN PRINCE OF DENMARK

Register membership and contribute "Insightful Observations" at
www.GuideToLaughing.com

Step One:

GETT
STA

ING
RTED

Why We do it

Arousal

Anatomy

WHY WE DO IT

Insightful Observations on
REASONS TO HAVE SEX

A little coitus never hoitus.

 Author Unknown

It's the most fun you can have without laughing.

 Woody Allen
(1935–) Director, Actor, Writer

Sexual intercourse is kicking death in the ass while singing.

 Charles Bukowski
(1920–1994) Writer, Poet

There are things that happen in the dark between two people that make everything that happens in the light seem all right.

 Erica Jong
(1942–) Writer, Poet

You must just acknowledge deep in your heart of hearts that people are supposed to fuck. It is our main purpose in life. All those other activities—playing the trumpet, vacuuming carpets, reading mystery novels, eating chocolate mousse—are just ways of passing time until you can fuck again.

 Cynthia Heimel
Present Day Writer, Humorist

Our bodies are shaped to bear children and our lives are a worship of the processes of creation. All ambition and intelligence are beside that great elemental point.

 Phyllis McGinley
(1905–1978) Author, Poet

12

WHY WE DO IT

Insightful Observations on
DEFINING SEX

Sex is an emotion in motion.

 Mae West
(1892–1980) Actress, Writer

The formula by which one and one makes three.

 Leonard L. Levinson
(1904–1974) Writer

Sex is a game, a weapon, a toy, a joy, a trance, an enlightenment, a loss, a hope.

 Sallie Tisdale
(1957–) Author, Editor

By the time he finishes defining sex, I think I'll learn that I'm actually a virgin.

 Scarlet Thomas
(1972–) Writer; **on Bill Clinton's definition during sex scandal.**

Sex is. There is nothing more to be done about it. Sex builds no roads, writes no novels, and sex certainly gives no meaning to anything in life but itself.

 Gore Vidal
(1925–) Novelist, Playwright, Essayist

The poor man's polo.

 Clifford Odets
(1906–1963) Playwright, Director, Actor

 = IDEALIST   = REALIST   = CYNIC

WHY WE DO IT

Insightful Observations on
EXPERIENCING SEX

The only thing better than sex is sex with chocolate on top.

Catherine Zeta-Jones
(1969–) Actress

I think sex is a part of everything. I don't think of sex as just something that happens now and then. I can't imagine writing without the feel of sex. I mean sex is a diffuse feeling. It diffuses everything and only once in a while would it be called sex.

Nelson Algren
(1909–1981) Novelist

Of the delights of this world, man cares most for sexual intercourse. He will go to any length for it—risk fortune, character, reputation, life itself.

Mark Twain
(1835–1910) Writer, Humorist

Some things are better than sex and some are worse, but there's nothing exactly like it.

W.C. Fields
(1879–1946) Actor, Screenwriter

What is sex? According to the women who love it, it includes all of our senses, and it also includes how we think and put information together; how we feel about what is happening and what it all means to us. If a partner is involved, it includes how we respond to our partner's sensations, thoughts, emotions, and meanings. Moreover, our sexual relationships occur in time, a time present that includes both time past and time future memories and dreams, terrors, anxieties, hopes, anticipations.

Dr. Gina Ogden
Present Day Psychologist, Sex Therapist, Author

14

WHY WE DO IT

Insightful Observations on
THE IMPORTANCE OF SEX

Time is short and we must seize,
These pleasures found above the knees.

😵 **English Folk Proverb**

The ability to enjoy your sex life is central. I don't give a shit about anything else. My obsession is total; what else is there to live for?

😵 **Dudley Moore**
(1935–2002) Actor,
Comedian, Writer, Musician

Sex is as important as eating or drinking and we ought to allow the one appetite to be satisfied with as little restraint or false modesty as the other.

😵 **Marquis de Sade**
(1740–1814) French Author

Sex is as important as a cheese sandwich. But a cheese sandwich, if you ain't got one in your belly, is extremely important.

😊 **Ian Drury**
(1943–2000) Musician

For all the pseudo-sophistication of twentieth-century sex theory, it is still assumed that a man should make love as if his principal intention was to people the wilderness.

😊 **Germaine Greer**
(1939–) Feminist, Writer,
Lecturer

Nothing in our culture, not even home computers, is more overrated than the epidermal felicity of two featherless bipeds in desperate congress.

😊 **Quentin Crisp**
(1908–1999) Writer

WHY WE DO IT

Insightful Observations on
HEALTH BENEFITS

Healthy lusty sex is wonderful.

 John Wayne
(1907–1979) Actor

A bit of lusting after someone does wonders for the skin.

 Elizabeth Hurley
(1965–) Actress

A healthy sex life—best thing in the world for a woman's voice.

 Leontyne Price
(1927–) Singer

I am convinced that happy, guiltless, and lusty intercourse stimulates the circulation and digestion, gets all the glands going, and is the best physical medicine in the world.

 Alan Watts
(1915–1973) Mystic, Lecturer

Only one percent of all heart attacks are triggered by sexual activity

 Graham Jackson
Present Day British Heart Specialist at St Thomas's Hospital in London

I think making love is the best form of exercise.

 Cary Grant
(1904–1986) Actor

The only time human beings are sane is the ten minutes after intercourse.

 Eric Berne
(1910–1970) Psychoanalyst

16

WHY WE DO IT

Insightful Observations on
LUST

If it is not erotic, it is not interesting.

 **Fernando Arrabal**
(1932–) Playwright, Novelist

Absolutely pure animal magnetism. Suddenly there was just the two of us. Everyone else melted away.

Tipper Gore
(1948–) Political Activist; **describing her first encounter with husband Al**

I want to do with you
What spring does
With the cherry trees

Pablo Neruda
(1904– 1973) Chilean Poet

Almost from day one, my feelings toward Florence were more carnal than maternal.

Barry Williams
(1954–) Actor; **on his stage mom Florence Henderson in** *The Brady Bunch*

Lust is what makes you keep wanting to do it, even when you have no desire to be with each other, even when you have no desire to do it.

Judith Viorst
(1931–) Author

I've looked at a lot of women with lust. I've committed adultery in my heart many times.

Jimmy Carter
(1924–) 29th U.S. President

WHY WE DO IT

Insightful Observations on
MORTALITY & SEX

Sex will outlive us all.

Samuel Goldwyn
(1879–1974) Movie Mogul

When people shout, "Oh, God! Oh, God! I'm coming!" while approaching orgasm, they are not bluffing. Sexual climax is as close as we get to God before our ultimate climax: death.

Phil Marquist
(1963–) Writer

Sex is one of the nine reasons of reincarnation. The other eight are unimportant.

Henry Miller
(1891–1980) Novelist

There is only one real antidote to the anguish engendered in humanity by it's awareness of inevitable death: erotic joy.

Benedikt Taschen
Publisher

Only death goes deeper than sex.

Mason Cooley
(1927–) Aphorist

Of the delights of this world, man cares most for sexual intercourse. Yet he has left it out of his heaven.

Mark Twain
(1835–1910) Writer, Humorist

WHY WE DO IT

Insightful Observations on
COMING OF AGE

My kid had sex with your honor student.

😆 Bumper sticker

If the young only knew; if the old only could.

😆 French Proverb

Young people are moving away from feeling guilty about sleeping with somebody to feeling guilty if they're not sleeping with somebody.

😉 Margaret Mead
(1901–1978) Anthropologist

Men are brought up to command, women to seduce.

😉 Sally Kempton
(1943–) Writer, Feminist

The first sexual stirring of little girls, so masked, so complex, so foolish as compared with the sex of little boys.

🙂 Lillian Hellman
(1905–1984) Playwright, Novelist

WHY WE DO IT

Insightful Observations on
BOYS COMING OF AGE

An erect penis has no brains.

 Morris Eigen
Businessman; **advice to his adolescent son**

Perhaps at fourteen every boy should be in love with some ideal woman to put on a pedestal and worship. As he grows up, of course, he will put her on a pedestal the better to view her legs.

 Barry Norman
(1933–) British Film Critic

I'm obsessed with girls. When you're my age your hormones are just kicking in and there's not much besides sex on your mind.

Leonardo DiCaprio
(1974–) Actor; **as a teenager**

In 2001, an Oklahoma couple was charged with tying their son to his bed to stop him from masturbating

 Sex, A Users Guide

The big mistake men make is that when they turn thirteen or fourteen and all of a sudden they've reached puberty, they believe that they like women. Actually, you're just horny. It doesn't mean you like women any more at twenty-one than you did at ten.

 Jules Feiffer
(1929–) Cartoonist, Playwright

WHY WE DO IT

Insightful Observations on
GIRLS COMING OF AGE

For what happened, of course, was totally to be foreseen. The great and terrible step was taken. What else could you expect from a girl so expectant? Sex, said Frank Harris, is the gateway to life. So I went through that gateway in an upper room in the Café Royal. That afternoon at the end of the session I walked back to Uncle Lexys at Warrington Crescent, reflecting on my rise. Like a corporal made sergeant.

Enid Bagnold
(1889–1981) Novelist, Playwrite

From the moment I was six, I felt sexy. And let me tell you it was hell, sheer hell, waiting to do something about it.

Bette Davis
(1908–1989) Actress

Because her need to love and be loved is smoldering and constant as a vestal fire, the young female is more randy than the male, whose lust rises and falls according to what is on offer.

Irma Kurtz
(1935–) Author

Quite a few women told me, one way or another, that they thought it was sex, not youth, that's wasted on the young.

Jean Harris
(1931–) Politician, Physician

= IDEALIST   = REALIST   = CYNIC

21

WHY WE DO IT

Insightful Observations on
BEING A WOMAN

If I have to, I can do anything. I am strong, I am invincible, I am woman.

Helen Reddy
(1941–) Singer, Songwriter
From "I Am Woman"

I don't know why women want any of the things that men have when one of the things that women have is men.

Coco Chanel
(1883–1971) Fashion Designer

"If God made anything better than a girl," Dover thought, "he sure kept it to himself."

Nelson Algren
(1909–1981) Novelist

One is not born but rather, one becomes a woman.

Simone de Beauvoir
(1908–1986) French
Existentialist, Writer

Females are naturally libidinous, incite the males to copulation, and cry out during the act of coition.

Aristotle
(384 BC–322 BC) Greek
Philosopher

Women are the only exploited group in history to have been idealized into powerlessness.

Erica Jong
(1942–) Writer, Poet

WHY WE DO IT

Insightful Observations on
BEING A MAN

On the one hand, we'll never experience childbirth. On the other hand, we can open all our own jars.

😉 **Bruce Willis**
(1955–) Actor, Producer, Composer, Singer

Tell me what a man finds sexually attractive and I will tell you his entire philosophy of life.

😉 **Ayn Rand**
(1905–1982) Novelist

See, the problem is that God gives men a brain and a penis, and only enough blood to run one at a time.

🙂 **Robin Williams**
(1952-) Comedian, Actor, Writer

God created man and finding him not sufficiently alone, gave him a companion to make him feel his solitude more keenly.

🙂 **Paul Valéry**
(1871–1945) Poet, Critic

Men wake up aroused in the morning. we can't help it. We just wake up and want you. And the women are thinking, "How can you want me the way I look in the morning?" It's because we can't see you. We have no blood anywhere near our optic nerve.

🙂 **Andy Rooney**
(1919–) Writer, Correspondent

WHY WE DO IT

Insightful Observations on
MALE DESIRE

Give me my golf clubs, fresh air and a beautiful partner, and you can keep my golf clubs and the fresh air.

Jack Benny
(1894–1974) Actor, Comedian

After two days in the hospital, I took a turn for the nurse.

W.C. Fields
(1879–1946) Actor, Screenwriter

DYAN CANNON: I know that you are in the mood. But honey, I'm not. Now do you want to do it, just like that, with no feeling on my part?
ELLIOTT GOULD: Yeah.

Bob & Carol & Ted & Alice
(1969) written by Paul Mazursky & Larry Tucker

Outside of every thin woman is a fat man trying to get in.

Katherine Whitehorn
(1928–) Columnist, Author

Men only have two feelings—we're either hungry or horny. I tell my wife, if I don't have an erection, make me a sandwich.

Bobby Slayton
(1951-) Comedian

As a guy, you're raised to get as much as you can. Sex, sex, sex, that's what you're after. After a while, I realized what I was doing was foolhardy. Still, it took some time to travel from the brain groinward.

Woody Harrelson
(1961–) Actor

There is no bigger fan of the opposite sex than me, and I have the bills to prove it.

Alan J. Lerner
(1918–1986) Lyricist, Playwright

THE GUIDE TO LAUGHING AT SEX

WHY WE DO IT

Insightful Observations on
FEMALE DESIRE

On a sofa upholstered in panther skin
Mona did research in original sin.

😵 **William Plomer**
(1903–1973) South African
Poet, Novelist

I find men terribly exciting and any girl who
says she doesn't is an old maid, a
streetwalker, or a saint.

😵 **Lana Turner**
(1920–1995) Actress

When you meet a man don't you always idly
wonder what he'd be like in bed? I do.

😊 **Helen Gurly Brown**
(1922–) Author, Editor

Sex is first of all a very visual thing. A man
walks through the door and I think, yes I
would, no I wouldn't. And any woman who says
she doesn't think that way, at least for a
second, is a liar.

😊 **Soraya Khashoggi**
wife of Arms Dealer Adnan
Khashoggi

The man's desire is for the woman; the
woman's desire is for the desire of the man.

😊 **Samuel Taylor
Coleridge**
(1772–1834) Poet

It's ill-becoming for an old broad to sing
about how bad she wants it. But occasionally
we do.

😊 **Lena Horne**
(1917–) Singer, Actress

WHY WE DO IT

Insightful Observations on
PASSION

They made love as though they were an endangered species.

 Peter De Vries
(1910–) Writer

Anyone can be passionate, but it takes real lovers to be silly.

 Rose Franklin
Writer

The only sin passion can commit is to be joyless.

 Dorothy Sayers
(1893–1957) Mystery Writer

The man who is master of his passions is reason's slave.

 Cyril Connolly
(1903–1974) British Journalist

Sexual passion is the cause of war and the end of peace, the basis of what is serious ... and consequently the concentration of all desire.

Arthur Schopenhauer
(1788–1860) German Philosopher

Men may love women, but they are in a rage with them, too. I believe it is a triumph of the human psyche that out of this contradiction, a new form of emotion emerges, one so human it is unknown to animals even one step lower in the evolutionary scale: passion.

Nancy Friday
(1937–) Writer, Psychologist

THE GUIDE TO LAUGHING AT SEX

WHY WE DO IT

Insightful Observations on
LESSONS FROM THE ANIMAL WORLD

Among the porcupines, rape is unknown.

😃 **Gregory Clark**
Author

The ability to make love frivolously is the chief characteristic which distinguishes human beings from beasts.

😃 **Heywood Broun**
(1888–1939) Journalist

Herodotus tells us that in cold countries beasts very seldom have horns, but in hot countires they have very large ones. This might bear a pleasant application.

😃 **Jonathan Swift**
(1667–1745) Clergyman, Satirist

I believe it was Galen who said that all animals are sad after coitus except for the female human and the rooster.

😉 **William Redfield**
(1921–1976) Actor

The kiss originated when the first male reptile licked the first female reptile, implying in a subtle, complimentary way that she was as succulent as the small reptile he had had for dinner the night before.

🙂 **F. Scott Fitzgerald**
(1896–1940) Author

AROUSAL

Insightful Observations on
SEX APPEAL

MALE DOG TO FEMALE DOG IN STREET: Boy, I'd love to meet you sometime off leash.

Mort Gerberg
Present Day Cartoonist in the *New Yorker*

I have always found strangers sexy.

Hugh Grant
(1960–) Actor

What is most beautiful in virile men is something feminine; what is most beautiful in feminine women is something masculine.

Susan Sontag
(1933-) Author, Director

I have heard the wish expressed that one could be a girl, and a good-looking girl, between the ages of thirteen and twenty-two, and after that become a man.

Jean de La Bruyere
(1645–1696) Author

Sex appeal is fifty percent what you've got and fifty percent what people think you've got.

Sophia Loren
(1934–) Actress

It was only after I got into show business that women started to like me. Before that I wasn't popular.

John Travolta
(1962–) Actor

28

AROUSAL

Insightful Observations on
FEMALE SEX APPEAL

With a binding like you've got, people are going to want to know what's in the book.

 **Gene Kelly**
to Leslie Caron in *An American in Paris* (1951)
written by Alan Jay Lerner

Men in lust aren't interested in quality.

Peter Nelson
Present Day Author

See, when a girl's under twenty-one, she's protected by law. When she's over sixty-five, she's protected by nature. Anywhere in between, she's fair game.

Cary Grant
in *Operation Petticoat* (1959)
written by Paul King & Joseph Stone

Men aren't attracted to me by my mind. They're attracted by what I don't mind.

Gypsy Rose Lee
(1914–1970) Dancer, Entertainer, Author

I'm not much interested in why it is that I find glasses on women sexy. ... Sensual pleasure—any kind of pleasure—calls out to be savored more than explained.

Charles Taylor
(1948–) Writer

I like the girls who do, I like the girls who don't;
I hate the girl who says she will and then she says she won't;
But the girl that I like best of all, and I think you'll say I'm right—
Is the one who says she never has, but looks as though she might.

Max Miller
(1894–1963) Writer, Actor

 = IDEALIST   = REALIST   😊 = CYNIC

29

AROUSAL

Insightful Observations on
MALE SEX APPEAL

I've noticed that as my reputation grows worse, my success with women increases.

Roman Polanski
(1933–) Director, Actor

Men ought to be more conscious of their bodies as an object of sexual desire.

Germaine Greer
(1939–) Feminist, Writer, Lecturer

I'd like to do a love scene with him just to see what all the yelling is about.

Shirley MacLaine
(1934–) Actress, Dancer, Writer; **on her brother Warren Beatty**

I refuse to go out with a man whose ass is smaller than mine.

Elizabeth Perkins
to Demi Moore in *About Last Night* (1986) written by Tim Kazurinsky & Denise DeClue, Play by David Mamet

AROUSAL

Insightful Observations on MALE AROUSAL

Male sexual response is far brisker and more automatic. It is triggered easily by things as simple as putting a quarter in a vending machine.

Dr. Alex Comfort
(1920–2000) British Writer,
Sexologist

Men thirty to thirty-nine years old think about sex every fifteen minutes. After forty, the frequency drops to once every half hour.

Men's Health
Magazine

I have to find a girl attractive or it's like trying to start a car without an ignition key.

Jonathan Aitken
(1910–1985) Newspaper
Publisher

In males, one of the most general causes of sexual excitement is constipation.... When this condition is chronic, as in habitual constipation, the unnatural excitement often leads to serious results.

Dr. J.H. Kellog
(1852–1943) Surgeon, Food
Reformer

Only in rare instances do women experience one tenth the sexual feeling which is familiar to men.

Dr. George Naphuys
Sex Authority in 1878

O, she is the antidote to desire.

William Congreve
(1670–1729) British
Dramatist

GETTING STARTED

AVOIDING SEX

EXPERIENCING SEX

EXPERIMENTING

COMMON PROBLEMS

SEX AND SOCIETY

AROUSAL

Insightful Observations on
FEMALE AROUSAL

I never dreamed that any mere physical experience could be so stimulating.

Katherine Hepburn
after surviving the rapids with Humphrey Bogart in *The African Queen* (1951)

PATRICIA NEAL: You look pretty good with your shirt off, you know. The sight of that through the kitchen window made me put down my dishtowel more'n once.

To Paul Newman
in *Hud* (1963) written by Harriet Frank Jr. and Larry McMurtry

He's interesting. But he's not Brazilian-bikini-wax interesting.

Marisa Acocella
Present Day Cartoonist in the *New Yorker*

I am not so easily aroused. For me, it takes quite a long time until the first kiss.

Jennifer Lopez
(1970–) Actress, Singer

If a woman is normally developed mentally, and well-bred, her sexual desire is small. If this were not so, the whole world would become a brothel and marriage and family impossible.

Joseph G. Ricahrdson, M.D.
Professor of Hygiene, University of Pennsylvania (1909 research)

AROUSAL

Insightful Observations on
THINKING ABOUT SEX

LEWIS ALANTE: Is sex all you ever think about?
SLADE BURRIS: Other thoughts creep in; I just ignore them.

Lewis Alante and Slade Burris
in *The Boys of Cellblock Q* (1992) written by Ralph Lucas, play by John C. Wall

A little theory makes sex more interesting, more comprehensible, and less scary—too much is a put down, especially as you're likely to get it out of perspective and become a spectator of your own performance.

Dr. Alex Comfort
(1920–2000) British Writer, Sexologist

He said that as a schoolboy sexual thoughts dominated his mind. I felt as I grew older this fever would lessen, even leave me. But it was not the case; it raged on through my twenties, and I thought: Well, surely by the time I am forty, I will receive some release from this torment, this constant search for the perfect love object.

But it was not to be; all through the forties it was lurking inside my head. And then I was fifty, and then I was sixty, and nothing changed: sexual images continued to spin around my brain like figures on a carousel. Now here I am in my seventies and I am still a prisoner of my sexual imagination. I'm stuck with it just at an age when I can no longer do anything about it.

E. M. Forster
(1879–1970) Writer, from Truman Capote's *Music for Chameleons*

A woman's mind is cleaner than a man's—that's because she changes it more often. Who knows, he's a man. You could lay your pussy on a table right in front of one and still not know what he's thinking.

Oliver Herford
(1863–1935) Author, Illustrator

To think is to say no.

Kim Cattrall
in HBO's *Sex and the City*

Emile Chartier
(1868–1951) French Writer

INSIGHTFUL OBSERVATIONS TO SHARE

33

AROUSAL

Insightful Observations on
EYE CONTACT

Words are only painted fire; a look is the fire itself.

 Mark Twain
(1835–1910) Writer, Humorist

When she raises her eyelids it's as if she were taking off all of her clothes.

 Colette
(1873–1954) French Novelist

Glances are the heavy artillery of the flirt: everything can be conveyed in a look, yet that look can always be denied, for it cannot be quoted word for word.

 Stendhal
(1885–1933) French Writer

Look at her. All over. Linger anywhere you like. When she notices (and she will if you're really looking), hold her eyes with yours. Hold them close. This is the essence of cruising, the experience that all the virtual reality and phone sex in the world will never replace. It is also the moment of truth. You'll know then and there whether she wants you or not.

 Susie Bright
(1958–) Writer, Editor

You know "that look" women get when they want sex? Me neither.

 Steve Martin
(1945–) Actor, Comedian, Writer

THE GUIDE TO LAUGHING AT SEX

AROUSAL

Insightful Observations on
SEX & SMELL

Exposure to pheromones is the essence of sex.

Dr. Winnifred Cutler
Biologist

Desperation.... It's the world's worst cologne.

Sheila Kelley
in *Singles* (1992) written by
Cameron Crowe

Insightful Observations on
SMELLING MEN

The best smell in the world is the smell of
the man that you love.

Jennifer Aniston
(1969–) Actress

Wear it anywhere you want to be touched.

Elizabeth Taylor
(1932–) Actress; **on
promoting her new cologne
for men**

Maybe if I hadn't been so fastidious, I might
have changed history. But, oh, that body
odor of his.

Lina Basquette
(1907–1994) Silent Film
Actress, **on Adolph Hitler's
attempt to seduce her.**

AROUSAL

Insightful Observations on
SMELLING WOMEN

The woman one loves always smells good.

 Remy de Gourmont
(1858–1915) French Poet,
Novelist, Critic

Her honeyish pungent female smell
monopolized the warm bed.

 John Updike
(1932–) Writer, Poet, Critic

There is nothing that smells so sweet as a
sweaty woman, especially if some of the
sweat on her is your own.

 Garrison Keillor
(1942–) Radio Host, Writer

The male gypsy moth can 'smell' the
virgin female gypsy moth from 1.8 miles
away.

 Author Unknown

To attract men I wear a perfume called
"New Car Interior."

 Rita Rudner
(1956–) Comedian

36

AROUSAL

Insightful Observations on
SEX & TOUCH

There is but one temple in the Universe ... and that is the human body. Nothing is holier than that high form. We touch heaven when we lay our hand on the human body.

 Thomas Carlyle
(1795–1881) British Historian

To lovers, touch is a metamorphosis. All the parts of their bodies seem to change, and seem to become something different and better.

 John Cheever
(1912–1982) Writer

Love is blind; that is why he always proceeds by the sense of touch.

 French Proverb

Woman talking to man on a date; "Don't touch me again—my body is rejecting you."

 Frank Cotham
Present Day Cartoonist in the *New Yorker*

 = IDEALIST   = REALIST   = CYNIC

AROUSAL

Insightful Observations on APPEARANCE

When beauty fires the blood, how love exalts the mind!

John Dryden
(1631–1700) British Poet

Bait: A preparation which renders the hook more palatable. The best kind is beauty.

Ambrose Bierce
(1842–1914) Writer

Any man who says he doesn't desire to have sex with a woman he thinks is attractive is lying.

Corbin Bernsen
(1954–) Actor

One of the paramount reasons for staying attractive is so you can have somebody to go to bed with.

Helen Gurly Brown
(1922–) Author, Editor

Beauty isn't everything! But then, what is?

Lanford Wilson
(1937–) Playwright

38

AROUSAL

Insightful Observations on
HAIR

Hair is another name for sex.

 Vidal Sassoon
(1928–) Hair Stylist, CEO

Being baldplate is an unfailing sex magnet.

 Telly Savalas
(1922–1994) Actor

Nudists who remove all their body hair are called "smoothies"

 Sex, A Users Guide

Leg hair is manly, chest hair is manly, but manliness can apparently only be expressed on one side of the body, because according to my sources, ass hair and back hair are unacceptable.

😃 **Natalie Krinsky**
Yale Univeristy Advice
Columnist

Insightful Observations on
LIPS

No other flesh like lip flesh! No meat like mouth meat! The musical clink of tooth against tooth! The wonderful curiosity of tongues!

 Tom Robbins
(1936–) Author

I love your lips when they're wet with wine
And red with a wicked desire.

 Ella Wheeler Wilcox
(1855–1919) Poet, Journalist

AROUSAL

Insightful Observations on CLOTHING

There is nothing more sensual than angora.

Ed Wood Jr.
(1924–1978) Movie Producer

What a man enjoys about a woman's clothes are his fantasies of how she would look without them.

Brendan Francis
(1923–1964) Irish Journalist, Dramatist

She was stark naked except for the PVC raincoat, dress, net stockings, undergarments, shoes, rainhat and gloves.

Keith Waterhouse
(1929–) British Playwrite

A dress has no meaning unless it makes a man want to take it off.

Francoise Sagan
(1935–) Novelist

Female clothing has been disappearing literally and philosophically.

Marilyn Bender
(1925–) *New York Times* Fashion Critic

Seamed stockings aren't subtle but they certainly do the job. You shouldn't wear them when out with someone you're not prepared to sleep with, since their presence is tantamount to saying, "Hi there, big fellow, please rip my clothes off at your earliest opportunity." If you really want your escort paralytic with lust, stop frequently to adjust the seams.

Cynthia Heimel
Present Day Writer, Humorist

40

AROUSAL

Insightful Observations on LINGERIE

Brevity is the soul of lingerie.

Dorothy Parker
(1893–1967) Writer

If love is blind, why is lingerie so popular?

Author Unknown

It is difficult to see why lace should be so
expensive; it's mostly holes.

Mary Wilson Little
Writer

Insightful Observations on HIGH HEELS

I don't know who invented the high heel, but
all women owe him a lot.

Marilyn Monroe
(1926–1962) Actress

When French and Italian men began to be
turned on to the female leg in decorative
high heels, they did not like to see the same
erotic footwear on the feet of men. All but
a few men stopped wearing high heels, which
went from being a man's standard footwear
to one of his favorite sexual fetishes.

Charles Panati
Present Day Author

AROUSAL

Insightful Observations on
APHRODISIACS

Love is it's own aphrodisiac and is the main ingredient for lasting sex.

Mort Katz
(1925–) Psychotherapist, Writer

If you paint the inside of your chicken coop orange, your chickens will lay more eggs.

Author Unknown

Power is the great aphrodisiac.

Henry Kissinger
(1923–) Political Scientist, Public Official

Erection is chiefly caused by scuraum, eringos, cresses, crymon, parsnips, artichokes, turnips, asparagus, candied ginger, acorns bruised to powder and drunk in muscatel, scallion, sea shellfish, etc.

Aristotle
(384BC–322BC) Greek Philosopher

Everything which inflames one's appetite is likely to arouse the other also. Pepper, mustard, ketchup and Worcestershire sauce—shun them all. And even salt, in any but the smallest quantity, is objectionable; it is such a goad toward carnalism that the ancient fable depicted Venus as born of the salt of sea-wave.

Dr. Dio Lewis
Expert on Women in 1874

It's not that I'm prudish. It's just that my mother told me never to enter any man's room in months that have an R.

Love Affair
(1939) Referring to the custom of eating oysters only in months with an R in the name.

AROUSAL

Insightful Observations on WATER

I would love to have sex all the time, even in the swimming pool. I don't care if it's the deep end or the shallow. I can work anyplace.

 Julio Iglesias
(1943–) Spanish Singer

I have observed, on board a steamer, how men and women easily give way to their instinct for flirtation, because water has the power of washing away our sense of responsibility, and those who on land resemble the oak in their firmness behave like floating seaweed when on the sea.

Rabindranath Tagore
(1861–1941) Bengali Poet, Philosopher

Fire (male sexuality) easily flares up but is easily extinguished by water; water (female sexuality) takes a long time to heat over the fire, but cools down very slowly.

I-Ching
Written by Chinese Emperor Fu Hsi (2958–2838 BC)

Water is sexy. People who are wet look inevitably more erotic and appealing than people who are dry.

Yvonne Fulbright
New York University Columnist

AROUSAL

Insightful Observations on
MONEY

My biggest sex fantasy is we're making love and I realize I'm out of debt.

Beth Lapides
Comedian

I don't care how rich he is—as long as he has a yacht, his own private railroad car, and his own toothpaste.

Marilyn Monroe
(1926–1962) Actress

I've seen a lot of ugly guys in the league [National Basketball Association] with beautiful women.

Grant Hill
(1972–) Professional Basketball player

You should never kiss a girl unless you have enough bucks to buy her a big ring and her own VCR 'cause she'll want to have videos of the wedding.

Jim, Age 10

When the Dow-Jones average goes up, the penis will too.

John O'Connor
(1920–2000) Catholic Official

I said I was worth a million. I didn't say I had millions.

Anthony Hayden-Guest
Present Day Writer, Jouranlist

44

ANATOMY

Insightful Observations on
GENITALIA

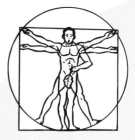

A straight man with a crooked penis is better than a crooked man with a straight one, and the right woman with the wrong vagina is better than the wrong woman with the right one.

 Eric Berne
(1910–1970) Psychoanalyst

The vagina is made so affable that it can accommodate itself to any penis, so that it will give way to a long one, meet a short one, widen to a thick one, constringe to a small one: so that every Man might well enough lie with any Woman, and every Woman with any Man.

 The Anatomy of Human Bodies
(Epitomised, 1682)

The human body must have been designed by a civil engineer. Who else would run a sanitary line through a recreation area?

 Author Unknown

Below the navel there is neither religion nor truth.

Italian proverb

😄 = IDEALIST   😊 = REALIST   🙂 = CYNIC

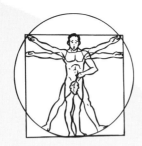

ANATOMY

Insightful Observations on
FEMALE GENITALIA

"The Grand Opening"

 Name of a Sex Shop for Women
Los Angeles, California

The human comedy begins with a vertical smile.

 Richard Condon
(1915–1996) ScreenWriter

… that wonderful rare space in you.

 Rainer Maria Rilke
(1875–1926) Lyric Poet

What's the definition of a vagina? The box a penis comes in.

 Andrew Dice Clay
(1958–) Comedian

Legs, I don't care if they're Greek columns or secondhand Steinways, what's between 'em is the passport to heaven. Yes, there are only two syllables in this whole wide world worth hearing: pus-sy.

 Al Pacino
in *Scent of a Woman* (1992)
written by Bo Goldman

It itself [the vagina] had an erotic appearance, like the inside of a giraffe's ear or a tropical fruit not much prized by the locals.

Kingsley Amis
(1922–1995) Novelist, Poet

I'm very uncomfortable with the idea of vaginas. They bother me in the same way that spiders bother some people.

 Boy George
(1961–) Singer, DJ

46

ANATOMY

Insightful Observations on
THE CLITORIS

Really that little deelybob is too far away from the hole. It should be built right in.

🙂 **Loretta Lynn**
(1935–) Country Singer,
Songwriter

The Victorians used the pearl as a euphemism for the clitoris and called an underworld pornographic magazine *The Pearl* for the association.

🙂 **Colin McDowell**
Present Day Author

Much like the stump end of a whist-card pencil.

🙂 **Dr. Marian Graves**
Medical Doctor

As women have known for a long time, the primary site for stimulation to orgasm centers on the clitoris. The revolution unleashed by the Kinsey Report of 1953 has, by now, made this information available to men who, for whatever reason, had not figured it out themselves by the more obvious routes of experience and sensitivity.

🙂 **Stephen Jay Gould**
(1941–2002) Paleontologist,
Author

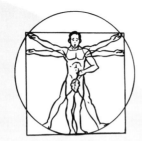

ANATOMY

Insightful Observations on
THE BUTTOCKS

The ass is the face of the soul of sex.

Charles Bukowski
(1920–1994) Writer, Poet

The shadow and substance of that warm divide that tends to drive all mankind to mutest adoration.

Gilbert Sorrentino
(1927–) Writer, Poet

I could not get over her butt, so I married her.

Robert Downey Jr.
(1965–) Actor, **on Deborah Falconer**

The most beautiful part of her long-sloping fall of the haunches from the socket of the back, and the slumberous round stillness of the buttocks. Like hillocks of sand the Arabs say, soft and downward-slipping with a long slope.

D.H. Lawrence
(1885–1930) Novelist, Poet, Essayist

The buttocks are the most aesthetically pleasing part of the body because they are nonfunctional. Although they conceal an essential orifice, these pointless globes are as near as the human form can ever come to abstract art.

Kenneth Tynan
(1927–1980) Theater Critic

ANATOMY

Insightful Observations on
BREASTS

Breasts and bosoms I have known,
Of varied shapes and sizes,
From poignant disappointments,
To jubilant surprises.

 Waldo Pierce
(1884–1970) Impressionist
Painter

She wore a short skirt and a tight sweater
and her figure described a set of parabolas
that could cause cardiac arrest in a yak.

 Woody Allen
(1935–) Director, Actor,
Writer

A pair of women's breasts has more pulling
power than a pair of oxen.

 Mexican Proverb

A full bosom is actually a millstone around a
woman's neck.... [Breasts] are not part of a
person but lures slung around her neck, to
be kneaded and twisted like magic, putty, or
mumbled and mouthed like lolly ices.

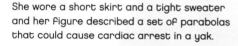 **Germaine Greer**
(1939–) Feminist, Writer,
Lecturer

I've met so many girls—"Here, feel these,
they're brand new." You grab them and
they're like bolt-ons—really hard. It's like
anything—it's got to be done just right.

 Steven Tyler
(1948–) Musician; **on breast
implants**

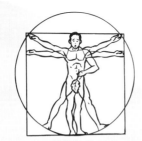

ANATOMY

Insightful Observations on
MALE GENITALIA

They're all different, like snowflakes.

 Margaret Cho
(1968–) Comedian, Actress

I'm thinking balls are to men what purses are to women. It's just a little bag, but we feel naked in public without it.

 Sarah Jessica Parker
in HBO's *Sex and the City*

Imagine ... hanging the stones of a man outside, where they are forever getting themselves knocked, pinched, and bruised. Any decent mechanic would have put them in the exact center of the body, protected by an envelope twice as thick as even a Presbyterian.

 H.L. Mencken
(1880–1956) Editor, Writer;
in a letter to William Manchester

A guy's penis is his whole life.

 Howard Stern
(1954–) Radio Personality,
on John Bobbitt, whose penis was cut off by his ex-wife

Men can't know what it's like to be pregnant, and women can't know what it's like to have an organ which is half involuntary. We're in a much better position to understand penises than you are, and we don't even know what's going on sometimes.

 Peter Nelson
Present Day Author

50

ANATOMY

Insightful Observations on
PENIS FACTS

Penis Facts:

1. The average penis is six inches long when erect.
2. Men live longer without their testicles. Men who are castrated have a life expectancy of thirteen years longer than do men with testicles.
3. The average male ejaculates approximately eighteen quarts of sperm in his lifetime.
4. The average man achieves an erection in less than ten seconds.
5. In one ejaculation there can be more than six hundred million sperm.
6. The average man can ejaculate nearly two feet.
7. The average teaspoon of semen contains five calories.

 Ron Louis & David Copeland
From *The Sex Lover's Book of Lists*

GETTING STARTED

AVOIDING SEX

EXPERIENCING SEX

EXPERIMENTING

COMMON PROBLEMS

SEX AND SOCIETY

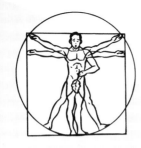

ANATOMY

Insightful Observations on
ERECTIONS

Schwing.

Mike Myers and Dana Carvey
in *Wayne's World* (1992) written by Mike Myers & Bonnie Turner

A stiff penis is nothing to be ashamed of.

Linda Lovelace
(1949–2002) Porn Star

Look at his basket. Hard as a steel baguette.

Mary Woronov
in *Scenes From the Class Struggle in Beverly Hills* (1989) Paul Bartel & Bruce Wagner

I'm glad I'm not a woman for a lot of reasons. Guys have a better deal.... Getting a hard-on, that's something a woman will never understand.

Christopher Walken
(1943–) Actor

An erection at will is the moral equivalent of a valid credit card.

Dr. Alex Comfort
(1920–2000) British Writer, Sexologist

Women think of being a man as a gift. It is a duty. Even making love can be a duty. A man has always got to get it up, and love isn't always enough.

Norman Mailer
(1923–) Writer

As tools, pricks aren't really reliable, one minute hard, the next pliable.

Fiona Pitt-Kethley
(1954–) Writer, Poet

52

ANATOMY

Insightful Observations on
PENIS SIZE

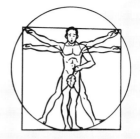

Michael was not a guy other guys would've made fun of in the locker room, okay?

 Bette Midler
in *Outrageous Fortune* (1987)
written by Leslie Dixon

His schlong brings to mind the fire hoses along the corridors at school. Schlong: the word somehow captures the brutishness, the meatiness that I admire so, the sheer mindless, weighty and unselfconscious dangle of that living piece of hose through which he passes water as thick and strong as rope.

Philip Roth
(1933–) Author

Thank you for your recent E-mail. I appreciate your concern. However, I am, at this time, completely satisfied with the size of my penis.

 Mick Stevens
Present Day Cartoonist in
the *New Yorker*

It's almost impossible to judge the size of an erect penis from its appearance in the flaccid state.

 Xaviera Hollander
(1943–) Madam, Writer

Beware of the man who denounces women writers.; his penis is tiny and he cannot spell.

 Erica Jong
(1942–) Writer, Poet

Some men say their erections aren't as big as they recall them once being. But then their partners say, "Well dear, you overestimated them back then too."

 Dr. Paul T. Costa Jr.
Expert on Personality and
Cognition; **on Male
Menopause**

 = IDEALIST   = REALIST = CYNIC

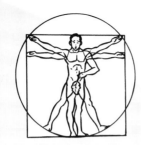

ANATOMY

Insightful Observations on PENIS ENVY

Okay, you want details? Okay. He's got the most perfect dick I've ever seen. Long, pink, amazing. It's dickalicious!

Kim Cattrall
in HBO's *Sex and the City*

I have a little bit of penis envy. Yeah, they're ridiculous, but they're cool.

K.D. Lang
(1962–) Singer, Songwriter

Contrary to Freud's theory, we do not envy the penis. The reasons are obvious. First, we would not know how to sit comfortably with one; second, we do not want something veiny falling out of our shorts; and third, a penis looks terrible in a tight dress.

Anka Radakovitch
Sex Columnist

Why is it that most things in the world are shaped like a man's penis?

Whoopi Goldberg
(1949–) Actress

No woman, except for the so-called "deviants" seriously wishes to be male and have a penis. But most women would like to have the privileges and opportunities that go with it.

Elena Gianini Belotti
Present Day Author

My problem is I'm both attracted and repelled by the male organ.

Diane Keaton
in *Manhattan* (1979) written by Woody Allen

54

ANATOMY

Insightful Observations on
NAMING THE PENIS

My boyfriend's penis is named "Captian Smiley," but I'm the one who named it. He [The Captain] sort of had a run in with a permanent marker while the boyfriend was sleeping.

Posted Online by
Melantha
August 2002

My boyfriend called his penis the "Devirginizer 2000"—sure lived up to it's name, the pervert. Anyway, it was called "DV" for short. Pun intended.

Author Unknown

Giving a name to the genitals may simply be an attempt to personify them but can also impute to them a life of their own, especially if their owner wishes to avoid responsibility for their actions.

Alan Richter
Writer

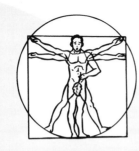

ANATOMY

Insightful Observations on
MAN & HIS PENIS

The penis is the only muscle man has that he cannot flex. It is also the only extremity that he cannot control.... But even worse, as it affects the dignity of its owner, is its seeming obedience to that inferior thing, woman. It rises at the sight, or even at the thought of a woman.

 Elizabeth Gould Davis
(1910–1974) Librarian, Writer

Women think of being a man as a gift. It is a duty. Even making love can be a duty. A man has always got to get it up, and love isn't always enough.

 Norman Mailer
(1923–) Writer

In good faith, 'a cares not what mischief he does, if his weapon be out: he will foin like any devil; he will spare neither man, woman nor child.

 William Shakespeare
(1564–1616) Playwright, Poet

March isn't the only thing that's in like a lion, out like a lamb.

 Author Unknown

Insightful Observations

_____

_____

_____

_____

_____

_____

_____

_____

_____

_____

_____

_____

_____

_____

_____

 = IDEALIST ☺ = REALIST ☺ = CYNIC

Step Two:

AVOIDI

ПG SEX

Sex Inhibitors

Alternatives to Sex

GETTING STARTED

AVOIDING SEX

EXPERIENCING SEX

EXPERIMENTING

COMMON PROBLEMS

SEX AND SOCIETY

SEX INHIBITORS

Insightful Observations on
ABSTINENCE

To me the term sexual freedom meant freedom from having to have sex.

 Jane Wagner
(1935–) Writer, Actress, Director

To me inspiration and creativity come only when I have abstained from a woman for a longish period. When, with passion, I have emptied my fluid into a woman until I am pumped dry, then inspiration shuns me. The same forces which go to fertilize a woman and create a human being go to create a work of art.

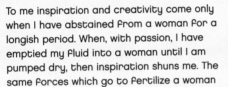 Frederic Chopin
(1810–1849) Composer

Celibacy is not hereditary.

 Oscar Wilde
(1854–1900) Poet, Playwright, Novelist

Abstinence is the mother of shameless lust.

 Pat Califia
(1959–) Writer, Activist

Sex as an institution, sex as a general notion, sex as a problem, sex as a platitude—all this is something I find too tedious for words. Let us just skip sex.

 Vladimir Nabokov
(1899–1977) Novelist

SEX INHIBITORS

Insightful Observations on
LOSING INTEREST

I'm at the age where food has taken the place of sex in my life. In fact, I've just had a mirror put over my kitchen table.

Rodney Dangerfield
(1921–) Actor, Comedian

Unless there's some emotional tie, I'd rather play tennis.

Bianca Jagger
(1950–) Ex-Wife of Mick Jagger

Dave lost interest in me and I lost interest in sex. I went shopping for gratification but that's like sex without a climax.

Bette Midler
in *Down and Out in Beverly Hills* (1986) written by Paul Mazursky & Leon Capetanos

Woman, observing that her mate went out of his way to make himself entertaining, rightly surmised that sex had something to do with it. From that she logically concluded that sex was recreational rather than procreational. (The small hearty band of girls who failed to get this point were responsible for the popularity of women's field hockey.)

James Thurber
(1894–1961) and E.B. White (1904–1971) authors of *Is Sex Necessary?*

 = IDEALIST   = REALIST   = CYNIC

61

SEX INHIBITORS

Insightful Observations on
INHIBITIONS & MODESTY

Oh, inhibitions are always nice because they're so nice to overcome.

 Jane Fonda
in *Klute* (1971) written by
Andy Lewis & Dave Lewis

Women have a special corner of their hearts for sins they have never committed.

 Cornelia Otis Skinner
(1901–1979) Stage Actress

Once you start having on-screen sex, it isn't embarrassing anymore.

 Annette Benning
(1958–) Actress

Something is wrong here: sex has been with us since the human race began its existence, yet I would estimate that ninety percent of human beings still suffer from enormous inhibitions in this area.

 Xaviera Hollander
(1943–) Madam, Writer

The daughter-in-law of Pythagoras said that a woman who goes to bed with a man ought to lay aside her modesty with her skirt, and put it on again with her petticoat.

 Michel de Montaigne
(1533–1592) French Essayist

SEX INHIBITORS

Insightful Observations on
DEFENDING REPUTATION

She's so pure, Moses couldn't even part her knees.

Joan Rivers
(1933–) Actress, Comedian

Paula Jones did not want her children to grow up thinking their mother was a slut.

Gil Davis
Attorney; **on why his client filed a sexual harassment lawsuit against Bill Clinton**

The odds are usually 2:1 in favor of sex. You and she against her conscience.

Evan Esar
(1899–1995) Writer

GILBERT ROLAND: I have heard so much about you.
MAE WEST: Yeah, but you can't prove it.

She Done Him Wrong
(1933)

A man can sleep around, no questions asked, but if a woman makes nineteen or twenty mistakes she's a tramp.

Joan Rivers
(1933–) Actress, Comedian

SEX INHIBITORS

Insightful Observations on
BAD REPUTATIONS

I like men who have a future and women who have a past.

Oscar Wilde
(1854–1900) Poet,
Playwright, Novelist

Now that I'm over sixty, I'm veering toward respectability.

Shelley Winters
(1922–) Actress

Until you've lost your reputation, you never realize what a burden it was or what freedom really is.

Margaret Mitchell
(1900–1949) Novelist

She's been on more laps than a napkin.

Walter Winchell
(1897–1972) Columnist,
Newscaster

If all the girls attending it [the Yale prom] were laid end to end, I wouldn't be surprised.

Dorothy Parker
(1893–1967) Writer

SEX INHIBITORS

Insightful Observations on
LOSS OF MORALITY

Eats first, morals after.

Bertolt Brecht
(1898–1956) Poet,
Playwright, Director

The older one grows the more one likes indecency.

Virginia Woolf
(1882–1941) British Novelist

I consider promiscuity immoral. Not because sex is evil, but because sex is too good and important.

Ayn Rand
(1905–1982) Novelist

As far as I'm concerned, morality is just a word that describes the current fashion of conduct.

Sally Stanford
(1903–1982) Madam, Vice-Mayor of Sausalito, California

The so-called new morality is the old immorality condoned.

Lord Shawcross
(1902–) British Lawyer, Politician

GETTING STARTED

AVOIDING SEX

EXPERIENCING SEX

EXPERIMENTING

COMMON PROBLEMS

SEX AND SOCIETY

SEX INHIBITORS

Insightful Observations on
RESISTING TEMPTATIONS

You cannot fight lust if you do not flee from the presence of men.

Sister of Saint
Caesarius of Arles
Founder of a 512 AD convent

The next time you feel the desire coming on, don't give way to it. If you have the chance, just wash your parts in cold water and cool them down.

Robert Baden-Powell
(1857–1941) British Soldier;
Founder of the Boy Scouts

I'll come no more behind your scenes, David; for the silk stockings and white bosoms of your actresses excite my amorous propensities.

Samuel Johnson
(1709–1784) British
Lexicographer; **said to
Actor-Manager David Garrick**

Sometimes in my dreams there are women.... When such dreams happen, immediately I remember, "I am a monk." ... It is very important to analyze "What is the real benefit of sexual desire?" The appearance of a beautiful face or a beautiful body—as many scriptures describe—no matter how beautiful, they essentially decompose into a skeleton. When we penetrate to its human flesh and bones, there is no beauty, is there? A couple in a sexual experience is happy for that moment. Then very soon trouble begins.

The Dalai Lama
(1935–) Tibetan Spiritual
Leader

Nothing in our culture, not even home computers, is more overrated than the epidermal felicity of two featherless bipeds in desperate congress.

Quentin Crisp
(1908–1999) Writer

SEX INHIBITORS

Insightful Observations on
WAITING

It isn't premarital sex if you have no intention of getting married.

 Matt Barry
Comedian

I am still a nice Jewish girl who believes in saving it for the wedding night.

 Ann Landers
(1918–2002) Advice Columnist

Give me chastity and continence. But not just now.

 St. Augustine
(1869–1945) 1st Archbishop of Canterbury

No sex is better than bad sex.

 Germaine Greer
(1939–) Feminist, Writer, Lecturer

No chupa, no shtupa—no wedding, no bedding.

 Yiddish Proverb

I keep making up these sex rules for myself and then I break them right away.

 Holden Caulfield
in *The Catcher In The Rye* written by J.D. Salinger (1919–) Author

SEX INHIBITORS

Insightful Observations on
SAYING "NO"

Not tonight Howard, but you have advanced to the next round.

New Yorker Cartoon
referring to *Who wants to be a Millionaire* gameshow.

Good thing I was not born a girl because I could never say no.

Warren G. Harding
(1865–1923) 29th U.S. President

A mutual and satisfied sexual act is of great benefit to the average woman, the magnetism of it is health giving. When it is not desired on the part of the woman and she has no response, it should not take place. This is an act of prostitution and is degrading to the woman's finer sensibility, all the marriage certificates on earth to the contrary notwithstanding.

Margeret Sanger
(1879–1916) Birth Control Pioneer

Tonight has been so perfect. Let's wait for another night to screw it up.

Janeane Garofalo
to Ben Chaplin in *The Truth about Cats and Dogs* (1996) written by Audrey Wells

Some of you who have already been around the block may have dabbled dangerously in sexual pleasure. It's time to straighten up and fly right. You're a wife and mother now—do you want people to think you're some disgusting slut? If you don't have a headache by now, start sniffing glue.

Susie Bright
(1958–) Writer, Editor

He says, "Come on honey. I can't remember the last time we made love."
She says, "Well I can and that's why we're not."

Rodney Dangerfield
(1921–) Actor, Comedian

68

SEX INHIBITORS

Insightful Observations on
MEN ON FRIGIDITY

She stood up, looked at me appraisingly, then closed all the drapes. And I made love to Joan Crawford, or, rather she made love to me. She was all business. She would put me on her calendar for the next visit.

Jackie Cooper
(1921-) Actor, Director

My wife is as cold as the hairs on a polar bear's butt.

Les Dawson
(1934–) British Comedian, Writer

I'm scared to death of the individual who has no sexual desires, no romantic desires, no fantasies.

John Cardinal O'Connor
(1920–2000) Catholic Prelate

My wife is the sort of woman who gives necrophilia a bad name.

Patrick Murray
Present Day Comedian

Madam, you have between your legs an instrument capable of giving pleasure to thousands—and all you can do is scratch it.

Sir Thomas Beecham
(1879–1961) Conductor; **to a woman cellist**

 = IDEALIST   = REALIST   = CYNIC

69

GETTING STARTED

AVOIDING SEX

EXPERIENCING SEX

EXPERIMENTING

COMMON PROBLEMS

SEX AND SOCIETY

SEX INHIBITORS

Insightful Observations on
WOMEN ON FRIGIDITY

I'm a born defroster.

 Jessica Lange
in *Tootsie* (1982)

I don't see so much of Alfred anymore since he got so interested in sex.

 Mrs. Alfred Kinsey
Wife of Sexuality
Researcher

When I hear his steps outside my door, I lie down on my bed, close my eyes, open my legs and think of England.

 Lady Alice Hillingdon
(1857–1940) **referring to sex with her husband**

After we made love he took a piece of chalk and made an outline of my body.

 Joan Rivers
(1933–) Actress, Comedian

I've tried several varieties of sex. The conventional position makes me claustrophobic, and the others either give me a stiff neck or lockjaw.

 Tallulah Bankhead
(1903–1968) Actress

THE GUIDE TO LAUGHING AT SEX

ALTERNATIVES TO SEX

Insightful Observations on
SEX SUBSTITUTIONS

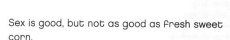

Sex is good, but not as good as fresh sweet corn.

 Garrison Keillor
(1942–) Radio Host, Writer

Shopping is better than sex. If you're not satisfied after shopping, you can make an exchange for something you really like.

 Adrienne Gusoff
(1953–) Writer

A sneeze absorbs all the functions of the soul as much as the sexual act.

🙂 **Blaise Pascal**
(1623–1662) Mathematician, Physicist, Theologian, Man-of-Letters

Next to the orgasm, a sneeze may be the closest thing there is in human eruption.

🙂 **Oscar Herman**
(1909–1980) Humorist, Shoe Salesman

For certain people, after fifty, litigation takes the place of sex.

🙂 **Gore Vidal**
(1925–) Novelist, Playwright, Essayist

GETTING STARTED

AVOIDING SEX

EXPERIENCING SEX

EXPERIMENTING

COMMON PROBLEMS

SEX AND SOCIETY

ALTERNATIVES TO SEX

Insightful Observations on
MASTURBATION

We have reason to believe that man first walked upright to free his hands for masturbation.

 Lily Tomlin
(1939–) Comedian, Actress

As per your specific question in regards to masturbation, I think that is something that is part of human sexuality and it's a part of something that perhaps should be taught [in public schools].

 Joycelyn Elders
(1933–) U.S. Surgeon General

Playing with oneself is a worthwhile activity for both sexes and one of the most rewarding of all the sexual practices. In terms of orgasmic efficacy, it seldom fails us. Alfred Kinsey reported that ninety five percent of the time it is successful, with seventy five percent of the participants attaining climax in less than four minutes.

 Lawrence Paros
Columnist, Author

I'm not weird or anything. I don't tie myself up first.

 Tom Waits
(1949–) Author, Composer, Actor

You are throwing away the seed that has been handed down to you as a trust instead of keeping it and ripening it for bringing a son to you later.

 Robert Baden-Powell
(1857–1941) British Soldier, Founder of the Boy Scouts

72

ALTERNATIVES TO SEX

Insightful Observations on
DISCOVERING MASTURBATION

Time sure flies when you're young and jerking off.

Leonardo Di Caprio
in *The Basketball Diaries* (1995) written by Bryan Goluboff, novel by Jim Carroll

I knew nothing at all about sex and simply thought that masturbation was a unique discovery on my part that was a lonely hobby of a sort that produced a pleasant sensation. I introduced it to my incredibly innocent prep school the next term—feeling like Marco Polo returning to Europe with the new inventions of gunpowder and paper— and soon the entire school was rocked to its foundations both metaphorically and physically.

Jeffrey Bernard
(1932–1997) English Writer

The first time I masturbated … it flew across the room and hit the far wall.

Jack Lemmon
(1925–2001) Actor

When I discovered it, I'd do it anywhere, I'd just whip it out and get on with it.

Oliver James
Author, Clinical Psychologist

When the habit is discovered, it must in young children be put a stop to by such means as tying the hands, strapping the knees together with a pad between them, or some mechanical plan.

Ada Ballin
Editor of *Baby Magazine*, London (1902)

INSIGHTFUL OBSERVATIONS TO SHARE

GETTING STARTED

AVOIDING SEX

EXPERIENCING SEX

EXPERIMENTING

COMMON PROBLEMS

SEX AND SOCIETY

ALTERNATIVES TO SEX

Insightful Observations on
MASTURBATION BENEFITS

We were poor. If I wasn't a boy, I wouldn't have had nothing to play with.

 Redd Foxx
(1922–1991) Comedian, Television Actor

Masturbation is the thinking-man's television

 Christopher Hampton
(1946–) British Playwright

I recommend masturbation because it's cheaper and you meet a better class of people that way.

 Buddy Hackett
(1924–2003) Actor, Comedian

Don't knock masturbation. It's sex with someone you love.

 Woody Allen
(1935–) Director, Actor, Writer

No minister, moralist, teacher, or scientific researcher has ever shown any evidence that masturbation is harmful in any way. Masturbation is fun.

 Dr. David Reuben
(1933–) Author; *Everything You Always Wanted to Know About Sex But Were Afraid to Ask*

THE GUIDE TO LAUGHING AT SEX

ALTERNATIVES TO SEX

Insightful Observations on
MASTURBATION & MORALITY

If God had intended us not to masturbate, He would have made our arms shorter.

😏 **George Carlin**
(1938–) Comedian, Actor, Writer

Masturbation: The primary sexual activity of mankind. In the nineteenth century it was a disease; in the twentieth, it's a cure.

😏 **Thomas Szasz**
(1920–) Psychiatrist

When the practice is begun at an early age, both mental and physical development may be notably interfered with. It is often stated that masturbation is a cause of insanity, epilepsy, and hysteria. I believe it to be more likely that masturbation is the first manifestation of a developing insanity.

🙂 **Dr. Charles Hunter Dunn**
Pediatrics Instructor at Harvard University from his 1920's Research

It is called in our schools 'beastliness', and this is about the best name for it … should it become a habit, it quickly destroys both health and spirits; he becomes feeble in body and mind, and often ends in a lunatic asylum.

🙂 **Robert Baden-Powell**
(1857–1941) British Soldier, Founder of the Boy Scouts; **referring to masturbation.**

The only difference between sex and death is, with death you can do it alone and nobody's going to make fun of you.

🙂 **Woody Allen**
(1935–) Director, Actor, Writer

Step Three:

EXPERI
SE

ENCING
X

Finding Sex

Foreplay

The Sex Act

Enjoying Sex

FINDING SEX

Insightful Observations on
SEX DRIVE

Great food is like great sex ... the more you have, the more you want.

 Gail Greene
New York Times Food Critic

Our biological drives are several million years older than our intelligence.

 Arthur E. Morgan
(1878–1976) Engineer,
Educator

The sex drive is nothing but motor memory of previously remembered pleasure.

 Wilhelm Reich
(1897–1957) Psychiatrist,
Author

In a new sex survey they found that eight percent of people had sex four or more times a week. Now here's the interesting part. That number drops to two percent when you add the phrase "With partner."

 David Letterman
(1947–) Humorist, Talk Show
Host

Guys would sleep with a bicycle if it had the right color lip gloss on. They have no shame. They're like bull elks in a field. It's a scent to them, a smell.

 Tori Amos
(1963–) Singer, Songwriter,
Musician

FINDING SEX

Insightful Observations on
HUNTING WOMEN

Man is the hunter; woman is his game:
The sleek and shining creatures of the
chase, We hunt them for the beauty of
their skins.

Alfred Lord
Tennyson
(1809–1892) British Poet

Hunt, pursue, and capture are biologically
programmed into the male sexuality.

Camille Paglia
(1947–) Author; Critic,
Educator

Easy sex, where a woman lies on a bed and
you get on top of her, isn't very interesting.
I'm a man, I like a struggle, a conquest. I just
happen to like being the loser, and then
made to satisfy the female winner.

Eric Stanton
(1926–1999) Erotic
Cartoonist

I don't think he has changed that much. He
still eyes a pretty lady—and why not? This is
part of his magnetism. This is Warren. What
has changed, I hope, is that he doesn't seem
to have that urge to bed these lovely ladies.
Now that is a major change.

Annette Benning
(1958–) Actress; **on
husband Warren Beatty**

SAMANTHA: If checking out other women is the
biggest problem you're having with him,
you're lucky.
CARRIE: Well, if it's that small, then he should
be able to stop.
SAMANTHA: Oh please, you can't change that
about a man. It's part of their genetic code.
Like farting.

Kim Cattrall and
Sarah Jessica
Parker
in HBO's *Sex and the City*

 = IDEALIST   = REALIST   = CYNIC

FINIDING SEX

Insightful Observations on
LURING MEN

When you want your boyfriend to play with you, wear a full-length black nightgown with buttons all over it. Sure, it's uncomfortable. But it makes you look just like his remote control.

Diana Jordan and Paul Seaburn
American Humorists

In a dear little village remote and obscure
A beautiful maiden resided,
As to whether or not her intentions were pure
Opinion was sharply divided.

Noel Coward
(1899–1973) English Actor, Dramatist, Songwriter

What else do women want in life but to be as attractive as possible to men? Do not all their trimmings and cosmetics have this end in view, and all their baths, fittings, creams, scents, as well—and all those arts of making up, painting and fashioning the face, eyes and skin. And by what other sponser are they better recommended to men than by folly?

Erasmus
(1469–1536) Dutch Priest, Humanist, Scholar

You don't do this to a person, you know. You don't walk around being fabulous when you know you're not available.

Billy Crystal
to Debra Winger in *Forget Paris* (1995) written by Billy Crystal, Lowell Ganz & Babaloo Mandel

80

FINDING SEX

Insightful Observations on
MALE SEX DRIVE

His sex beat about like the cane of a furious blind man.

Amos Oz
(1939–) Novelist

If I felt any better, I'd be flying. I don't need Viagra. I need the opposite, man. I'm hornier than a toad.

Jack Lalanne
(1914–) Fitness Pioneer; **at age 85**

You come out of a woman and you spend the rest of your life trying to get back inside.

Heathcote Williams
(1942–) Humorist

If you put a guy on a desert island, he'd do it to mud. A girl doesn't understand this: "You'd do it to the mud—you don't love me!" Sex is a different emotion.

Lenny Bruce
(1925–1966) Comedian

Man has a small organ. The more he feeds it, the more it needs, and vice versa.

The Talmud

I don't go through an hour a day when I don't get turned on.

Jack Nicholson
(1937–) Actor, Screenwriter, Producer, Director

GETTING STARTED

AVOIDING SEX

EXPERIENCING SEX

EXPERIMENTING

COMMON PROBLEMS

SEX AND SOCIETY

FINDING SEX

Insightful Observations on
FEMALE SEX DRIVE

Looking for some hot stuff, baby, this evening. I need some hot stuff, baby, tonight.
I want some hot stuff, baby, this evening.
Gotta have some hot stuff.
Gotta have some love tonight.

Donna Summer
"Hot Stuff," words and music by Pete Bellotte, Harold Faltermayer & Keith Forsey

One day she was sitting on the porch and I said, "Granny, how old does woman get before she don't want no more boyfriends?" (She was around 106 then.) She said, "I don't know Honey. You have to ask someone older than me."

Jackie "Moms" Mabley
(1894–1975) Comedian

The female sex drive is sixty percent vanity, thirty percent curiosity, and ten percent physical.

Florence King
(1936–) Author

If I still had a cherry, it would have been pushed back so far I could use it for a tail-light.

Nell Kimball
(1854–1934) American Madam

FINDING SEX

Insightful Observations on
LOVER QUALIFICATIONS

Anyone who's a great kisser I'm always interested in.

😵 Cher
(1946–) Actress, Singer

The perfect lover is one who turns into a pizza at 4:00 A.M.

😵 Charles Pierce
(1926–1999) Actor, Nightclub Performer

What most men desire is a virgin who is a whore.

😵 Edward Dahlberg
(1900–1977) Writer

I'm looking for a woman with an intense sexual appetite because I don't ever want to have to cheat.

😵 David Keith
(1954–) Actor

WILLIAM HURT: I need tending. I need someone to take care of me. Someone to rub my tired muscles, smooth out my sheets.
KATHLEEN TURNER: Get married.
WH: I just need it for tonight.

😊 Body Heat
(1981) written by Lawrence Kasdan

The number one rule of the road is never go to bed with anyone crazier than yourself. You will break this rule and you will be sorry.

😊 Kris Kristofferson
(1936–) Singer, Songwriter, Actor

GETTING STARTED

AVOIDING SEX

EXPERIENCING SEX

EXPERIMENTING

COMMON PROBLEMS

SEX AND SOCIETY

FINDING SEX

Insightful Observations on
MARRIED MEN

I enjoy dating married men because they don't want anything kinky, like breakfast.

 Joni Rodgers
Present Day Author

Avoiding married men totally when you're single would be like passing up first aid in a Tijuana hospital when you're bleeding to death because you prefer an immaculate American hospital.

 Helen Gurley Brown
(1922–) Author, Editor

I say I don't sleep with married men, but what I mean is I don't sleep with happily married men.

😏 **Britt Ekland**
(1942–) Swedish Film Actress

If I ever want to have an affair with a married man again, especially if he's the president, please shoot me.

🙂 **Monica Lewinsky**
(1973–) Former White House Intern

It's never easy keeping your own husband happy. It's much easier to make someone else's husband happy.

🙂 **Zsa Zsa Gabor**
(1917–) Hungarian Actress

84

FINDING SEX

Insightful Observations on
SEDUCING WOMEN

A woman's chastity consists, like an onion, of a series of coats.

😵 **Nathaniel Hawthorne**
(1804–1864) Writer

Nothing worth knowing can be understood with the mind. Everything really valuable has to enter you through a different opening.

😵 **Woody Allen**
(1935–) Director, Actor, Writer

A woman's most erogenous zone is her mind.

😊 **Raquel Welch**
(1940–) Actress, Sex Symbol,

It is not enough to conquer; one must know how to seduce.

😊 **Voltaire**
(1694–1778) French Writer, Philosopher

Do not insult a woman before she has undressed.

😊 **African Proverb**

A maid that laughs is half taken.

😊 **English Proverb**

She's harder to get into than a Pearl Jam concert.

😊 **Jack Noseworthy**
in *The Brady Bunch Movie* (1995)

FINDING SEX

Insightful Observations on
SEDUCING MEN

You can seduce a man without taking anything off, without even touching him.

 Rae Dawn Chong
(1962–) Actress

Want to get your paws full of honey, you sad funny bear?

 Mary Woronov
in *Scenes from the Class Struggle in Beverly Hills* (1989) Paul Bartel & Bruce Wagner

Men play the game; women know the score.

 Roger Woddis
Present Day Writer

The game women play is men.

 Adam Smith
(1723–1790) Economist, Moral Philosopher

The most romantic thing a woman ever said to me in bed was, "Are you sure you're not a cop?"

 Larry Brown
Comedian

The quickest way to a man's heart is through his chest.

 Roseanne Barr
(1952–) Actress, Comedian, Talk Show Host

FINDING SEX

Insightful Observations on
PROPOSITIONING WOMEN

Everything seems like nothing to me now. Except that I want you in my bed. I don't care if I burn in hell. I don't care if you burn in hell. The past and the future is a joke to me now. I see that they're nothing. I see they ain't here. The only thing that's here is you and me.

 Nicolas Cage
to Cher in *Moonstruck* (1987)
written by John Patrick Shanley

He offered his honor, she honored his offer, and all through the night, it was on her and off her.

 American Folk Rhyme

MAN HITS ON WOMAN AT BAR: "Would it help if I told you how moved I was by 'The Vagina Monologues'?"

 Lee Lorenz
Present Day Cartoonist in the *New Yorker*

Though a lady repel your advance, she'll be kind • Just as long as you intimate what's on your mind. • You may tell her you're hungry, you need to be swung, • You may ask her to see how your etchings are hung. • You may mention the ashes that need to be hauled; • Put the lid on her sauce-pan, but don't be too bold; • For the moment you're forthright, get ready to duck— • The girl isn't born yet who'll stand for Let's fuck!"

 Author Unknown
Ode to Four Letter Words

Paula Jones is suing President Clinton for $700,000 for allegedly proposing she perform a sex act on him. In that case, every woman in America is owed millions by construction workers.

 Elayne Boosler
(1952–) Comedian

 = IDEALIST   = REALIST   = CYNIC

FINDING SEX

Insightful Observations on
PROPOSITIONING MEN

Roy, what if I told you that I wasn't really your mother?

😵 **Anjelica Huston**
to John Cusack in *The Grifters* (1990) written by Donald E. Westlake, novel by Jim Thompson

My right leg is Christmas and my left leg is Thanksgiving. Why don't you come and visit me between the holidays?

😵 **Mae West**
(1892–1980) Actress, Writer

I always feel so selfish sleeping alone in a double bed when there are people in China sleeping on the ground.

😵 **Barbra Streisand**
to George Segal in *The Owl and the Pussycat* (1970) written by Buck Henry, play by Bill Manhoff

Don't know if I'm going to be able to sleep. Hint, hint.

😊 **Karen Black**
to Jack Nicholson in *Five Easy Pieces* (1970) written by Carole Eastman & Bob Rafelson

ELLEN BURSTYN: So, wanna fuck?
ALAN ALDA: What?
EB: You didn't understand the question?

😊 *Same Time, Next Year*
(1978) written by Bernard Slade

It's going to be a long night ... and I don't particularly like the book I started.

😊 **Eva Marie Saint**
to Cary Grant in *North by Northwest* (1959) written by Ernest Lehman

FINDING SEX

Insightful Observations on
LINES FOR MEN

You can either watch me or join me. One of them's more fun.

Peter O'Toole
in *My Favorite Year* (1982)
written by Dennis Palumbo
& Norman Steinberg

You have perfection about you. Your eyes have music. Your heart's the best part of your body. And when you move, every man, woman, and child is forced to watch.

Keith Carradine
to Lesley Ann Warren in
Choose Me (1884) written
by Alan Rudolph

Ask, and ask sexy. Say "can I kiss you?" or "I'm feeling like we oughta take off all our clothes, grind our genitals together for twenty or so minutes, then hop back in the shower for a rinse and some cunnilingus, then jump back in bed, eat some Ben & Jerry's Cherry Garcia and then maybe have another go at it. How are you feeling?"

Dan Savage
Sex-Advice Columnist

Despite his appearance, he enjoyed a considerable sexual success among suggestible college girls, whom he would approach with the honest unappealing inquiry, Can I jump you?

Brendan Gill
(1914–1997) Author,
Preservationist; **on Dylan
Thomas**

I tell the women that the face is my experience and the hands are my soul—anything to get those panties down.

Charles Bukowski
(1920–1994) Writer, Poet

GETTING STARTED

AVOIDING SEX

EXPERIENCING SEX

EXPERIMENTING

COMMON PROBLEMS

SEX AND SOCIETY

FINDING SEX

Insightful Observations on DATING & SEX

The three F's of dating: One: Film. Two: Food. Three: Fuck.

Kevin Pollak
(1957–) Actor; **on the bachelor's credo**

A man on a date wonders if he'll get lucky. The woman already knows.

Monica Piper
Present Day Humorist, Television Writer

Men generally pay for all expenses on a date … Either sex, however, may bring a little gift, its value to be determined by the bizarreness of the sexual request to be made later in that evening.

P.J. O'Rourke
(1947–) Humorist, Journalist

On a date … I wonder if there is going to be any sex—and if I'm going to be involved.

Garry Shandling
(1949–) Actor, Writer, Comedian

The only thing that went down on Charlotte's dates with any regularity was an American Express Gold card.

Sarah Jessica Parker
in HBO's *Sex and the City*

I went out with this one guy; I was very excited about it. He took me out to dinner; he made me laugh—he made me pay. He's like, "Oh, I'm sorry. I forgot my wallet." "Really? I forgot my vagina."

Lisa Sundstedt
Comedian

90

FINDING SEX

Insightful Observations on
ONE-NIGHT STANDS

Hey, this girl does not have one-night stands. Every guy I have ever slept with—and we are way into double digits here—has come back for more. Every single one!

Bette Midler
in *Outrageous Fortune* (1987)

I'm always looking for meaningful one-night stands.

Dudley Moore
(1935–2002) Actor, Comedian, Writer, Musician

If we end up together, then this is the most romantic day of my whole life. And if we don't, then I'm a complete slut.

Kathleen Turner
to Michael Douglas in *The War of the Roses* (1989) by Michael Leeson, novel by Warren Adler

I did not sleep. I never do when I am over-happy, over-unhappy, or in bed with a strange man.

Edna O'Brien
(1932–) Novelist, Short-Story Writer

I'm not the type of guy who enjoys one-night stands. It leaves me feeling very empty and cynical. It's not even fun sexually. I need to feel something for the woman and entertain the vain hope that it may lead to a relationship.

Ben Affleck
(1972–) Actor, Writer

FINDING SEX

Insightful Observations on
THE MORNING AFTER

A man has missed something if he has never woken up in an anonymous bed beside a face he'll never see again, and if he has never left a brothel at dawn feeling like jumping off a bridge into the river out of sheer physical disgust with life.

Gustave Flaubert
(1821–1880) French Writer

It's best to move the scene away from the bedroom rather soon so he can see you in a different way. Take him to the kitchen or, if you are going to chat, the living room.... Give him real coffee instead of instant.

Helen Gurley Brown
(1922–) Author, Editor

The glances over cocktails,
That seem to be so sweet.
Don't seem quite so amorous,
Over Shredded Wheat.

Frank Muir
(1920–) Writer,
Broadcaster

The great thing about ships that pass in the night is they don't stay for breakfast. In fact, I don't know which I like more, the sound of them coming, or the sound of them going.

Barry Creyton
Present Day Playwrite

DEAN BASTOUNES (ONE NIGHT STAND): So what's for breakfast?
ELIZABETH PERKINS: Egg McMuffin. Corner of Broadway and Belmont.

About Last Night
(1986) written by Tim Kazurinsky & Denise DeClue, Play by David Mamet

92

FINDINGSEX

Insightful Observations on
SEX AT WORK

If women can sleep their way to the top, how come they aren't there?

😊 Ellen Goodman
(1941–) Newspaper Columnist

As for not sleeping with the boss, why discriminate against him?

😊 Helen Gurley Brown
(1922–) Author, Editor

Employees make the best dates. You don't have to pick them up and they're always tax deductible.

😊 Andy Warhol
(1928–1987) Pop Artist, Filmmaker

BOSS TALKING TO EMPLOYEE IN HIS OFFICE: "It's come to my attention that you've been using our internet access to troll for babes."

🙂 Robert Mankoff
Present Day Cartoonist in the *New Yorker*

She's the kind of girl who climbed the ladder to success, wrong by wrong.

🙂 Mark Twain
(1835–1910) Writer, Humorist

GETTING STARTED

AVOIDING SEX

EXPERIENCING SEX

EXPERIMENTING

COMMON PROBLEMS

SEX AND SOCIETY

FINDING SEX

Insightful Observations on STRIP CLUBS

It's about time that people forget that image of strip clubs as seedy places.... Rather, today's strip clubs are capital-intensive female-empowerment zones.

 Demi Moore
(1962–) Actress, Producer

Strippers are generally open minded.... Whatever you want, they'll say, "All right." Sex is so matter-of-fact with them.

 Drew Carey
(1958-) Actor, Writer, Comedian

At the strip clubs, I pay a ten-dollar cover. A beautiful nude woman dances inches away from my face, I can't touch her, she can't touch me, I can't touch myself, and I give her all my money. You know that's what hell has to be like.

 Jeff Garlin
(1962–) Writer, Comedian

Women now have the right to plant rolled-up dollar bills in the jockstraps of steroid-sodden male strippers.

 Howard Ogden
Humorist; on the emergence of strip clubs for women clientele

94

FINDING SEX

Insightful Observations on
BUYING SEX

I believe that sex is the most beautiful, natural, and wholesome thing money can buy.

Steve Martin
(1945–) Actor, Comedian, Writer

I enter a whorehouse with the same interest as I do the British Museum or the Metropolitan—in the same spirit of curiosity. Here are the works of man, here is the art of man, here is his eternal pursuit of gold and pleasure. I couldn't be more sincere.

Errol Flynn
(1909–1959) Actor

The big difference between sex for money and sex for free is that sex for money usually costs a lot less.

Brendan Francis
(1923–1964) Irish Journalist, Dramatist

There is only one other profession that outranks bankers as dedicated clients, and that is the stockbroker. When the stocks go up, the cocks go up!

Xaviera Hollander
(1943–) Madam, Writer

I never turned over a fig leaf that didn't have a price tag on the other side.

Saul Bellow
(1915–) Canadian Writer

In love, you pay as you leave.

Mark Twain
(1835–1910) Writer, Humorist

 = IDEALIST   = REALIST   😊 = CYNIC

GETTING STARTED

AVOIDING SEX

EXPERIENCING SEX

EXPERIMENTING

COMMON PROBLEMS

SEX AND SOCIETY

FINDING SEX

Insightful Observations on SELLING SEX

Our hookers don't do it out of obligation, or necessity. Here, prostitution doesn't occur for that reason, but because, somehow, they like it.

Fidel Castro
(1927–) Cuban Revolutionary, Political Leader

Prostitution seems to be a problem. But what's the problem? Fucking is okay. Selling is okay. So why isn't selling fucking okay?

George Carlin
(1938–) Comedian, Actor, Writer

Men need to be despunked regularly. It's when they're not getting a regular despunking that they start causing problems. I call that a service, not a nuisance.

Cynthia Payne
(1932–) Madam

If widgets sold as well as sex, I would sell widgets. But nothing seems to sell as fast as sex.

Seth Warshavsky
(1973–) Internet Porn Tycoon

Why is it immoral to be paid for an act that is perfectly legal if done for free?

Glorian Allred and Lisa Bloom
Mother-Daughter Writing Team

Sex is the great amateur art. The professional, male or female, is frowned upon; he or she misses the point and spoils the whole show.

David Cort
(1904–1983) Writer

FINDING SEX

Insightful Observations on
HOOKER DATES

Are you a hooker? Jesus, I forgot. I just thought I was doing great with you.

Dudley Moore
in *Arthur* (1981) written by Steve Gordon

I think I can truthfully say that my behavior in whorehouses has been exemplary.

Errol Flynn
(1909–1959) Actor

When I was a call girl, men were not paying for sex. They were paying for something else. They were paying to act out a fantasy or they were paying for companionship or they were paying to be seen with a well-dressed young woman. Or they were paying for someone to listen to them.... What I did was no different from what ninety-nine percent of American women are taught to do. I took the money from under the lamp instead of in Trade.

Roberta Victor
Former Prostitute

I appreciate this whole seduction scene you've got going here, but let me give you a tip: I'm a sure thing.

Julia Roberts
to Richard Gere in *Pretty Woman* (1990) written by J.F. Lawton

What do you mean, 'Not tonight, I have a headache'? You're a prostitute.

Robert Mankoff
Present Day Cartoonist in the *New Yorker*

FOREPLAY

Insightful Observations on
KISSING

A word invented by the poets as a rhyme for bliss.

Ambrose Bierce
(1842–1914) Writer

He kissed the plump mellow smellow melons of her rump, on each plump melonous hemisphere, in their mellow yellow furrow, with obscure prolonged provocative melonsmelonous osculation.

James Joyce
(1882–1941) Writer, Poet

Kisses may not spread germs, but they certainly lower resistance.

Louise Erickson
in, *Reader's Digest*, May 1949

There are three kinds of kissers: The fire extinguisher, the mummy, and the vacuum cleaner.

Helen Gurley Brown
(1922–) Author, Editor

A kiss is an application for a better position.

Jeff Rovin
(1951–) Writer

I've kissed so many women I can do it with my eyes closed.

Henny Youngman
(1906–1998) Comedian

A man who can't kiss can't fuck.

Cynthia Heimel
Present Day Writer, Humorist

98

FOREPLAY

Insightful Observations on
FOREPLAY

Mrs. Robinson, do you think we could say a few words to each other first this time?

😵 **Dustin Hoffman**
to Anne Bancroft in *The Graduate* (1967) written by Calder Willingham & Buck Henry, novel by Charles Webb

If you suck on his fingers, you'd better not be kidding.

😉 **Cynthia Heimel**
Present Day Writer, Humorist

Dancing is the perpendicular expression of horizontal desire.

😉 **Author Unknown**

Don't stint on foreplay, be inventive.

😉 **Dr. Ruth Westheimer**
(1928–) Psychologist, Author, Sex Counselor

The 1950s were ten years of foreplay.

😊 **Germaine Greer**
(1939–) Feminist, Writer, Lecturer

Women prefer thirty to forty minutes of foreplay. Men prefer thirty to forty seconds of foreplay. Men consider driving back to her place as part of the foreplay.

😊 **Matt Groening**
(1954–) Writer, Humorist, Cartoonist

INSIGHTFUL OBSERVATIONS TO SHARE

FOREPLAY

Insightful Observations on
HAND JOBS

Good lovers have known for centuries that the hand is probably the primary sex organ.

 Eleanor Hamilton
Writer, Poet

Shaking hands with Bill Clinton is, in and of itself, a full body sexual experience, I promise you. He has the sexiest handshake of any man that I have ever experienced in my life.

 Judith Krantz
(1928–) Novelist

In some parts of New Gunea, pulling someone's penis is a sign of goodwill.

 Sex, A User's Guide
written by Stephen Arnott

Fondling a man's privates is *not* like testing peaches in the supermarket.

 Cynthia Heimel
Present Day Writer,
Humorist

No one gives hand jobs anymore. I've asked around. I find this highly alarming. I understand that this might seem a little strange; I mean, most girls do not even know how to give hand jobs.

 Natalie Krinsky
Yale Univeristy Columnist

100

FOREPLAY

Insightful Observations on ORAL SEX

Love makes the world go down.

😈 Graffiti

Never do with your hands what you could do better with your mouth.

😈 Cherry Vanilla
(1943–) Rock Groupie, Poetess

Graze on my lips; and if those hills be dry, Stray lower, where the pleasant fountains lie.

😈 William Shakespeare
(1564–1616) Playwright, Poet

SAMANTHA: Going down, giving head …
CARRIE: Eating out …
MIRANDA: I never understood that. Shouldn't it be "eating in?"

😉 HBO's *Sex and the City*

You know the worst thing about oral sex? The view.

🙂 Maureen Lipman
(1946–) English Actress, Writer

Sometimes a cigar is just a cigar.

🙂 Sigmund Freud, MD
(1856–1939) Founder of Psychoanalysis; **on phallic dream symbolism**

Soixante-neuf, or 69, commonly considered the Pike's Peak of sexual positioning is anatomically unsound, if not unnatural. Despite love-manual hymns of the joy of simultaneous head giving, the technique leaves much to be desired. Sixty-nine will always be a crowd pleaser in bed, but it's still an ass-backwards way of getting off.

🙂 Philip Nobile
Journalist, Author

FOREPLAY

Insightful Observations on
MEN PERFORMING ORAL SEX

Some men love oral sex. ... If you find a man like this, treat him well. Feed him caviar and don't let your girlfriends catch a glimpse of him.

Cynthia Heimel
Present Day Writer, Humorist

Some men know that a light touch of the tongue, running from a woman's toes to her ears, lingering in the softest way possible in various places in between, given often enough and sincerely enough, would add immeasurably to world peace.

Marianne Williamson
(1952–) Spiritualist, Writer

Many women have the gut feeling that their genitals are ugly. One reason women are gratified by oral genital relations is that is a way of saying I like your cunt. I can eat it.

Erica Jong
(1942–) Writer, Poet

Made a hell of a discovery the other night. Eyelashes on the clit ... can blink her off in no time.

Dan Jenkins
(1929–) Novelist, Journalist

Older guys like to receive head, but they don't like to give it.

Victoria Principal
(1946–) Actress

102

FOREPLAY

Insightful Observations on
WOMEN PERFORMING ORAL SEX

The cure for starvation in India and the cure for overpopulation—both in one big swallow.

 **Erica Jong**
(1942–) Writer, Poet

Oral sex is a great way to tone up your cheekbones.

Cynthia Heimel
Present Day Writer,
Humorist

I never understood what he saw in her until I saw her eating corn on the cob at the Caprice.

Carol Browne
(1913–1991) Stage Actress,
Comedian

No Phillipa—suck! "Blow" is just an expression.

English Folk Saying

I wouldn't want the whole world to know how I do it.... I had to spend three or four weeks learning how to keep from gagging, and how to breathe with the strokes.

Linda Lovelace
(1949–2002) Porn Star in
Deep Throat; **on her oral technique**

A man I once met said, "There's a yin and yang to giving head: the yin being the mouth, the yang being the hand, and, tragically, girls never have enough yang."

Rachael Klein
University of California,
Berkeley Columnist

= IDEALIST   = REALIST   = CYNIC

GETTING STARTED

AVOIDING SEX

EXPERIENCING SEX

EXPERIMENTING

COMMON PROBLEMS

SEX AND SOCIETY

FOREPLAY

Insightful Observations on
UNDRESSING A WOMAN

Let me take you a button hole lower.

 William Shakespeare
(1564–1616) Playwright, Poet

Madame, shall we undress you for the fight?
The wars are naked that we make tonight.

 George Moore
(1852–1933) Novelist, Poet, Playwright

For a woman to be loved, she usually ought to be naked.

 Pierre Cardin
(1922–) Fashion Designer

According to a new survey, women say they feel more comfortable undressing in front of men than they do undressing in front of other women. They say that women are too judgmental, where, of course, men are just grateful.

Author Unknown

FOREPLAY

Insightful Observations on DISROBING

Take off the shell with your clothes.

 Dr. Alex Comfort
(1920–2000) British Writer,
Sexologist

I just look in the mirror and I say God, it's really fantastic, the Lord really gave me something. So why on earth should I cover any of it up?

 Edy Williams
(1942–) "B" Movie Actress

When you sleep with someone you take off a lot more than your clothes.

Anna Quindlen
(1952–) Author, Journalist

If it was the fashion to go naked, the face would be hardly observed.

Lady Mary Wortley Montagu
(1689–1762) Writer

Full-frontal nudity ... has now become accepted by every branch of the theatrical profession with the possible exception of lady accordion-players.

 Dennis Norden
Present Day British Humorist

If God had wanted us to walk around naked, we would have been born that way.

 Author Unknown

FOREPLAY

Insightful Observations on
BEING NAKED

It's not true that I had nothing on. I had on the radio.

Marilyn Monroe
(1926–1962) Actress

There was an old sculptor named Phidias
Whose knowledge of Art was invidious.
He carved Aphrodite, Without any nightie
Which startled the purely fastidious.

Author Unknown

Historically, bathing nude
Was never in the least bit rude.
The Greeks, who cannot be construed,
As ever being crass or crude,
Would swim and dive and fish for food.
Mama, Papa and all the brood,
Caught crabs and eels and ate them stewed
And then, replete in festive mood,
Sweet music played and maidens wooed.
No parsimonious prying prude,
Quoting St Justin or St Jude
Accused the Greeks of being lewd.
That just was not the attitude.

Ronnie Barker
(1929–) Writer, Actor

To be naked is to be oneself.
To be nude is to be seen naked by others,
and yet not recognized for oneself....
Nudity is a form of dress.

John Berger
(1926–) Artist, Poet,
Screenwriter

106

THE SEX ACT

Insightful Observations on
LOST VIRGINITY

I used to be Snow White ... but I drifted.

Mae West
(1892–1980) Actress, Writer

I'll wager you that in ten years it will be fashionable again to be a virgin.

Barbara Cartland
(1901–2000) British
Romance Novelist

Loss of virginity is rational increase; and there was never virgin got till virginity was first lost.

William Shakespeare
(1564–1616) Playwright, Poet

We may eventually come to realize that chastity is no more a virtue than malnutrition.

Dr. Alex Comfort
(1920–2000) British Writer,
Sexologist

How has it happened, what have we come to that the Scarlet Letter these days isn't an A, but V?

Joyce Maynard
(1953–) Novelist, Political
Commentator; **on virginity**

Nature abhors a virgin—a frozen asset.

Clare Booth Luce
(1903–1987) Playwright,
Journalist, U.S.
Congresswoman

INSIGHTFUL OBSERVATIONS TO SHARE

GETTING STARTED

AVOIDING SEX

EXPERIENCING SEX

EXPERIMENTING

COMMON PROBLEMS

SEX AND SOCIETY

THE SEX ACT

Insightful Observations on
FIRST TIME EXPERIENCES, MEN

The first girl you go to bed with is always pretty.

 Walter Matthau
(1920–2000) Actor, Director

Receiving this honor is without a question one of the greatest moments of my life, second only to that magical evening, backstage in Shelley Winters' dressing room, where I first became a man.

 Martin Short
(1950–) Actor, Humorist;
upon receiving an honorary degree

I was so naive I didn't know where to put my peter. I was trying to put it in her belly button. After we finally did it, I felt so bad that I had sinned, I cried, I went to the Father and confessed.

 Billy Martin
(1928–) Baseball Player, Manager

Then we got over into the back seat of the car, fumbling and feeling and scrambling for each other and I couldn't get it up.

 Bob Guccione
(1930–) *Penthouse* Publisher

108

THE SEX ACT

Insightful Observations on
FIRST TIME EXPERIENCES, WOMEN

I was horny and I enjoyed it a lot. Balling is always good and sometimes it just knocks your brains out. The first time you ball somebody is always excellent.

😆 **Grace Slick**
(1939–) 60's Rock Icon

It takes a lot of experience for a girl to kiss like a beginner.

😏 *Ladies Home Journal*
1948

Losing my virginity was a career move.

😏 **Madonna**
(1958–) Singer, Songwriter, Actress

I was crying and crying. When he started to spread my legs I went into a fit. I cried and screamed. I thought it was just a little thing and it stayed one size. I couldn't pee without hurting for a month.

🙂 **Loretta Lynn**
(1935–) Country Singer, Songwriter

GARY BROCKETTE: You a virgin?
CYBILL SHEPHERD: Yes, I am.
GB: Too bad.
CS: I don't want to be, though.
GB: I don't blame you. Come see me when you're not.

🙂 *The Last Picture Show*
(1971) written by Larry McMurtry

THE SEX ACT

Insightful Observations on LATE BLOOMERS

I was a virgin 'til I was twenty, and then again 'til I was twenty-three.

  Carrie Snow
Actress, Writer

I was pretty old before I had my first sexual experience. The reason is that I was born by caesarian section and had no frame of reference.

  Jeff Hilton
Comedian

This is very unusual. I've never been alone with a man before—even with my dress on. With my dress off, it's most unusual.

  Audrey Hepburn
(1929–1993) to Gregory Peck in *Roman Holiday* (1953) written by Ian McLellan Hunter & John Dighton

You have opened up the prison gates of my womanhood. And all the passion that was unsatisfied in me for so many years, leaped into a wild reckless storm boundless as the sea.

  Emma Goldman
(1869–1940) Letter to Ben Reitman

110

THE SEX ACT

Insightful Observations on SEX ON THE FIRST DATE

If you take my heart by surprise, the rest of my body has the right to follow.

🙂 **Albert Finney**
in *Tom Jones* (1963) written by John Osborne, novel by Henry Fielding

Sure it was a perfect stranger. But strangers are the only perfect people I know.

🙂 **Anthony Hayden-Guest**
Present Day Writer, Journalist

A date is a job interview that lasts all night. The only difference between a date and a job interview is that there aren't many job interviews where there's a chance you'll end up naked at the end of it.

🙂 **Jerry Seinfeld**
(1954–) Comedian, Actor

Never, ever go to bed with a man on the first date. Not ever. Unless you really want to.

😌 **Cynthia Heimel**
Present Day Writer, Humorist

🙂 = IDEALIST   😌 = REALIST   🙂 = CYNIC

THE SEX ACT

Insightful Observations on
THE SEX ACT

I'd like to meet the man who invented sex and see what he's working on now.

Author Unknown

There is nothing that impairs a man's sexual performance quicker than any suggestion that he's not doing it right.

Helen Lawrenson
(1907–1982) Writer, Editor

Sex is like having dinner: sometimes you joke about the the dishes, sometimes you take the meal seriously.

Woody Allen
(1935–) Director, Actor, Writer

Whatever else can be said about sex, it cannot be called a dignified performance.

Helen Lawrenson
(1907–1982) Writer, Editor

The position is ridiculous, the pleasure momentary, the expense damnable.

Lord Chesterfield
(1694–1773) British Writer

Sex is not some sort of pristine, reverent ritual. You want reverence and pristine, go to church.

Cynthia Heimel
Present Day Writer, Humorist

THE SEX ACT

Insightful Observations on CASUAL SEX

All this talk about sex, all this worry about sex—big deal. The sun makes me happy. I eat a good fish, it makes me happy. I sleep with a good man, he makes me happy.

Melina Mercouri
(1923–1994) Film Actress

Sex without love is an empty experience. But as empty experiences go, it's one of the best.

Woody Allen
(1935–) Director, Actor, Writer

Love is the answer, but while you are waiting for the answer, sex raises some pretty good questions.

Woody Allen
(1935–) Director, Actor, Writer

Sex without love is just two people masturbating together.

John Holmes
(1944–1988) Porn Star

Ducking for apples—change one letter and it's the story of my life.

Dorothy Parker
(1893–1967) Writer

When I think of some of the men I've slept with—if they were women, I wouldn't have had lunch with them.

Carol Siskind
Present Day Actress, Comedian

It's too much trouble to get laid. Because you have to go out with a guy, and go to dinner with him, and listen to him talk about his opinions. And I don't have that kind of time.

Kathy Griffin
(1964–) Actress, Comedian

THE SEX ACT

Insightful Observations on
EMOTIONAL CONNECTIONS

If you have sex and you know you've made the other person happy, it's so much better than doing it for yourself. Although if you're using your left hand, it's really like you're doing it with someone else.

 Jim Carrey
(1962–) Actor, Comedian

Sex is a conversation carried out by another means.

 Peter Ustinov
(1921–) British Writer, Actor

You don't get high-quality sex without love.

 Dr. Alex Comfort
(1920–2000) British Writer, Sexologist

The intimacy in sex is never only physical. In a sexual relationship we may discover who we are in ways otherwise unavailable to us, and at the same time we allow our partner to see and know that individual. As we unveil our bodies, we also disclose our persons.

 Dr. Thomas Moore
Theologian, Writer

MARGARET COLIN: I thought sentiment made you uncomfortable.
TOM SELLECK: I can handle it, as long as it's disguised as sex.

 Three Men and a Baby
(1987) written by Jim Cruickshank & James Orr

114

THE SEX ACT

Insightful Observations on
SEX SOUNDS

Isn't it interesting how the sounds are the same for an awful nightmare and great sex?

 Rue McClanahan
(1935–) Actress

Let's pull back the covers and be frank here. Sex is about moistness, and moistness creates a world of sound that you may not wish to hear in your living room. People want passion, not sounds of plumbing in distress.

 Sandi Toksvig
British Comedian

INSIGHTFUL OBSERVATIONS TO SHARE

THE SEX ACT

Insightful Observations on
MANNERS

Always treat a lady like a whore and a whore like a lady.

Wilson Mizner
(1876–1933) Actor, Writer

Southerners will forgive anybody anything if they have good manners. Once, a particularly charming Congressman who had been a guest at a church dinner my mother had attended was caught sometime later rather, well, flagrantly, as the French would say, in a motel room wearing a dog collar and his wife's lace bra and panties. Mother's response when asked if she would vote for him again? "Why, of course. After all, everybody's got their little quirks. Besides he has lovely table manners."

Fannie Flagg
(1944–) Actress, Writer

Those people who think good sex is more important to a marriage than good manners will find they are wrong.... In bed, the two most erotic words in any language are "thank you" and "please."

Hubert Downs
Writer

It would be rude to get your sexual satisfaction by tying someone to the bed and then leaving him or her there and going out with someone more attractive.

P.J. O'Rourke
(1947–) Humorist, Journalist

At a swing party, I say it's bad etiquette to be the first to take out a whip. One should wait for the host or hostess to do so first. Don't you agree?

Dr. Marty Klein
Marriage Counselor, Sex Therapist; **on favorite questions he's been asked about sex.**

116

THE SEX ACT

Insightful Observations on
TALKING DURING SEX

MAN IN BATHROBE APPROACHING WOMAN IN BED: "I thought I'd start things off with the 'shock and awe' phase of the operation."

J.C. Duffy
Present Day Cartoonist in the *New Yorker*

A man wrote me about his girlfriend. Whenever they had sex, she liked to talk finance. She'd say things like, "Come on, baby, let's see you balance my checkbook," or "Oh, honey. Take a loan out for my apartment and pay no interest for six months." Once she shouted, "Mortgage my house payment NOW!"

Deb Levine
Ask Delilah Advice Columnist

I don't say anything during sex. I've been told not to. Told during sex in fact.

Chevy Chase
(1943–) Actor, Comedian

Oral sex is currently very trendy. It is even preferred to the regular kind. It is preferred because it's the only way most of us can get our sex partners to shut up.

P.J. O'Rourke
(1947–) Humorist, Journalist

Baby talk is not an aphrodisiac.

Cynthia Heimel
Present Day Writer, Humorist

GETTING STARTED

AVOIDING SEX

EXPERIENCING SEX

EXPERIMENTING

COMMON PROBLEMS

SEX AND SOCIETY

THE SEX ACT

Insightful Observations on
LAUGHING DURING SEX

What isn't funny about sex?

 Roz Warren
Writer, Editor

Sex is identical to comedy in that it involves timing.

Phyllis Diller
(1917–) Comedian, Actress, Author

Its okay to laugh in the bedroom so long as you don't point.

Will Durst
Modern Day Humorist

What makes sex funny and love not? Love is unfunny. There are no jokes about people falling in love, but there are plenty about people getting laid.

Natalie Krinsky
Yale University Advice Columnist

Sex and laughter do go very well together, and I wondered—and still do—which is the more important.

Hermione Gingold
(1897–1987) British Actress, Writer

If men knew what women laughed about, they would never sleep with us.

Erica Jong
(1942–) Writer, Poet

118

THE SEX ACT

Insightful Observations on
DEFINING ORGASMS

The sex orgasm has a poetic power, like a comet.

Joán Miró
(1893–1983) Artist

What is an orgasm, after all, except laughter of the loins.

Mickey Rooney
(1920–) Movie Actor

Death is orgasm is rebirth is death is orgasm.

William S. Burroughs
(1914–1997) Author

There can be back of the neck orgasms, bottom of the foot orgasms, and palm of the hand orgasms.

Masters and Johnson
Twentieth Century Human Sexuality Researchers, Authors

I have come to think of orgasms as the things that I have really quickly while the guy gets up to look in the refrigerator for something to drink.

Merrill Markoe
Present Day TV Writer; *Late Night with David Letterman*

 = IDEALIST = REALIST = CYNIC

THE SEX ACT

Insightful Observations on
EXPERIENCING AN ORGASM

Like the tickling feeling you get inside your nose before you sneeze.

 Sex Manual for Teens

It may be discovered someday that an orgasm actually lasts for hours and only seems like a few seconds.

 Dolly Parton
(1946–) Singer, Songwriter, Actress

Electric flesh-arrows ... traversing the body. A rainbow of color strikes the eyelids. A foam of music falls over the ears. It is the gong of the orgasm.

 Anais Nin
(1903–1977) French Author

A great portion [of semen] comes from the brain.

 Ambrose Pare
(1510–1590) French Battlefield Surgeon

What do atheists scream when they come?

 Bill Hicks
(1961–1994) Comedian

Now I know what I've been faking all these years.

 Goldie Hawn
in *Private Benjamin* (1980)

THE GUIDE TO LAUGHING AT SEX

THE SEX ACT

Insightful Observations on
FEMALE ORGASMS

So the female orgasm is simply a nervous climax to sex relations ... It may be thought of as a sort of pleasure-prize that comes with a box of cereal. It is all to the good if the prize is there, the cereal is valuable and nourishing if not.

 Madeline Gray
Present Day Author

I haven't had an orgasm like that in nine and a half years. I never thought I was capable of this. I'm ashamed of myself. I am. Glad and ashamed.

Bette Midler
in *Down and Out in Beverly Hills* (1986) written by Paul Mazursky & Leon Capetanos

Fully one half of all women seldom or never experience any pleasure whatever in the sexual act. Now this is an impeachment of nature, a disgrace to our civilization.

Victoria Woodhull
(1838–1927) First Woman Nominated For U.S. President

Much contention and strife will arise in that house where the wife shall get up dissatisfied with her husband.

 Sa'di Gulistan
(1206–1291) Poet, Philosopher

In the case of some women, orgasms take quite a bit of time. Before signing on with such a partner, make sure you are willing to lay aside, say, the month of June, with sandwiches having to be brought in.

 Bruce Jay Friedman
(1930–) Author, Humorist

THE SEX ACT

Insightful Observations on
SEX ON THE WEDDING NIGHT

Lovemaking is a sublime art that needs practice if it's to be true and significant. But I suspect you're going to be an excellent student.

Charlie Chaplin
(1889–1977) Actor, Director, Writer; **on deflowering his bride**

The day after that wedding night, I found that a distance of a thousand miles, abyss and discovery and irremediable metamorphosis, separated me from the day before.

Colette
(1873–1954) French Novelist

Said a newly-wed maiden of Ealing,
"A honeymoon seems so appealing
But for nearly two weeks, I've heard only bed-squeaks,
And seen nothing but cracks in the ceiling."

Author Unknown

A new bride should be treated like a new car. Keep her steady on straight, watch out for warning lights on the ignition and lubrication panels and then, when you reckon she's run in, give her all you've got.

Auberon Waugh
(1938–) British Author

These days, the honeymoon is rehearsed much more often than the wedding.

P.J. O'Rourke
(1947–) Humorist, Journalist

THE SEX ACT

Insightful Observations on
SEX WHILE PREGNANT

Making love in the morning got me through morning sickness—I found I could be happy and throw up at the same time.

  Pamela Anderson Lee
(1967–) Model, Actress; **on being pregnant**

MIRANDA: Okay I reeeeeaaaally need to have sex with him now. Next time he gets back in town I'll be too big and he won't want to. Nothing puts a man off sex like pregnancy. This is my last chance. Last chance for sex.
CARRIE: You're not on death row.
MIRANDA: Yes I am. Dead woman fucking.

Cynthia Nixon and Sarah Jessica Parker
in HBO's *Sex and the City*

ENJOYING SEX

Insightful Observations on
EXPERIENCING PLEASURE

No man is a hypocrite in his pleasures.

Samuel Johnson
(1709– 1784) British
Lexicographer

Everyone is dragged on by their favorite pleasure.

Virgil
(70–19 B.C.) Roman Poet

Pleasure is the object, the duty, the goal of all rational creatures.

Voltaire
(1694–1778) French Writer,
Philosopher

What does "good in bed" mean to me? When I'm sick and I stay home from school propped up with lots of pillows watching TV and my mom brings me soup—that's good in bed.

Brooke Shields
(1965–) Actress, Model

There is no greater nor keener pleasure than that of bodily love—and none which is more irrational.

Plato
(427–348 BC) Greek
Philosopher

All the things I really like to do are either immoral, illegal, or fattening.

Alexander Woollcott
(1887– 1943) Journalist

THE GUIDE TO LAUGHING AT SEX

ENJOYING SEX

Insightful Observations on
AVOIDING BAD SEX

Bad sex is only bad if you let it be.

 Meghan Bainum
University of Kansas Sex
Columnist

There's nothing better than good sex. But bad sex? A peanut butter and jelly sandwich is better than bad sex.

Billy Joel
(1949–) Singer, Songwriter

The art of pleasing consists in being pleased.

William Hazlitt
(1778–1830) British Essayist

If sex is a pain in the ass, then you're doing it wrong.

Rodney Dangerfield
(1921–) Actor, Comedian

You're a boring fuck.

Joan Collins
(1933–) Actress; to Arthur
Loew when he accused her
of being a "fucking bore"

ENJOYING SEX

Insightful Observations on
VARIETY

Variety is the one simple and foolproof aphrodisiac

 Author Unknown

If all we have to choose from is the limp dick or the super hard dick, we're in trouble. We need a versatile dick who admits that intercourse isn't all there is to sexuality, who can negotiate rough sex on Monday, eating pussy on Tuesday and cuddling on Wednesday.

 Bell Hooks
(1952–) Writer

There's a story about President and Mrs. Coolidge visiting a poultry show. The guide says to Mrs. Coolidge, "You know, Ma'am, the rooster here performs his services up to eight or nine times a day." To which the First Lady replied, "Please see to it that the President is given that information!" A while later the President's party came through the same exhibit and the guide told him, "Sir, Mrs. Coolidge said to be sure to tell you that the rooster there performs his services up to eight or nine times a day." Coolidge thought for a moment and asked, "Same chicken each time?" "No, Mr. President, different chickens each time." "Then see to it that Mrs. Coolidge is given that information!"

 Author Unknown

The last time I tried to make love with my wife nothing was happening so I said to her, "What's the matter, you can't think of anybody either?"

 Rodney Dangerfield
(1921–) Actor, Comedian

126

ENJOYING SEX

Insightful Observations on
SEX SKILLS

Having sex is like playing bridge. If you don't have a good partner, you'd better have a good hand.

😊 **Woody Allen**
(1935–) Director, Actor, Writer

If I were asked for a one-line answer to the question, "What makes a woman good in bed?" I would say, "A man who is good in bed."

😊 **Bob Guccione**
(1930–) *Penthouse* Publisher

Sexuality education is a lifelong process of acquiring information and forming attitudes, beliefs and values about identity, relationships and intimacy. It encompasses sexual development, reproductive health, interpersonal relationships, affection, intimacy, body image and gender roles.

😊 **Sexual Information and Education Council of the United States**

Remember, if you smoke after sex you're doing it too fast.

😊 **Woody Allen**
(1935–) Director, Actor, Writer

Sex is the great amateur sport. The professional, male or female, is frowned upon; he or she misses the whole point and spoils the show.

🙂 **David Cort**
(1904–1983) Writer

😊 = IDEALIST   😊 = REALIST   🙂 = CYNIC

127

GETTING STARTED
AVOIDING SEX
EXPERIENCING SEX
EXPERIMENTING
COMMON PROBLEMS
SEX AND SOCIETY

ENJOYING SEX

Insightful Observations on
MALE SEX SKILLS

You made a woman meow?

Bruno Kirby
in *When Harry Met Sally* (1989)
written by Nora Ephron

To see, taste, touch, hear and smell the essence of a woman is to become a successful explorer, a modern Jacques Cousteau, a teacher and an A-plus student, all at the same time.

Dylan Edwards
Writer

I'm very much in touch with my feminine side.... Women don't always want to be manhandled. A lot of times they want to be made love to by a man who can do it softly, like a woman.

Luke Perry
(1965–) Actor

If you want to really test your sex skills, try the "Rodeo Fuck." It's when you are doing your girl from behind, then you bend over and whisper your secretary's name in her ear and try to hold on for eight seconds.

Brooke Temple
(1940–) Entrepreneur

A slow thrust should resemble the movement of a carp caught on the hook; a quick thrust should resemble the flight of birds against the wind. Inserting and withdrawing, moving up and down and from left to right ...

Li Tung-Hsuan
(646–740) Author; *The Art of Love*

If you want to watch porn, that's your business, but I wouldn't be taking notes down for technique tips.

Teresa Chin
University of California, Berkeley Sex Columnist

It's so easy where it is and men never seem to be able to find it. You're like, "It's right there!" When they do find it, you wish they hadn't because they're really rough ... they're pushing it like it's an elevator button.

Jennifer Tilly
(1958–) Actress

128

ENJOYING SEX

Insightful Observations on
BAD MALE LOVERS

I'm not a great lover, but at least I'm fast.

Drew Carey
(1958-) Actor, Writer, Comedian

So many guys who can assemble a refrigerator for you, guys who can take apart your computer and put it back together again, guys who can fix your dishwasher, have no idea where anything is on a woman. Why can't we just give everyone, when we meet them, some sort of a manual, like you would when you buy a Cuisinart?

Merrill Markoe
Present Day TV Writer;
Late Night with David Letterman

The male attitude toward sex is like squirting jam into a doughnut.

Germaine Greer
(1939-) Feminist, Writer, Lecturer

SAMANTHA: Is he that bad in bed?
MIRANDA: No. He's just ... he's a guy. He can rebuild a jet engine but when it comes to a woman.... What's the big mystery? It's my clitoris, not the Sphinx.

Kim Cattrall and Cynthia Nixon
in HBO's *Sex and the City*

ALEXANDRA: "Old Faithful" couldn't even rise to the occasion!
GEORGE: Even if I could, I would've needed a crowbar to gain entry.
ALEXANDRA: A bad workman always blames his tools.

Barry Creyton
Present Day Playwrite

I'm a terrible lover. I've actually given a woman an anti-climax.

Scott Roeben
(1965-) Writer

WELLNESS THROUGH LAUGHTER

ENJOYING SEX

Insightful Observations on
FEMALE SEX SKILLS

I do give a good blow job. I really, really do, and I wish you could get a grade, or some type of certificate. I realized I was really good at it, I guess, when I was 20 or 21 years old. I was giving a blow job, and he said, "You do this so well. What are you going to do with the rest of your life?"

 Ellen Cleghorne
(1965–) Comedian

Given half a chance, a woman offers her whole being. It's instinctive with her. Not a man! A man is always more muddled than a woman. He needs a woman if for no other reason than to be straightened out. Sometimes it takes nothing more than a good, clean, healthy fuck to do the trick.

Henry Miller
(1891–1980) Novelist

I swear people don't want sex so much as they want somebody who'll listen to 'em ... the first thing you learn after fellatio is how to listen.

Jane Wagner
(1935–) Writer, Actress, Director

It is naïve in the extreme for women to be regarded as equals by men so long as they persist in subhuman (i.e., animal-like) behavior during sexual intercourse; I'm referring to the outlandish PANTING, GASPING, MOANING, SOBBING, WRITHING, SCRATCHING, BITING, SCREAMING, and the seemingly invariable OH MY GOD. ... All so predictably integral to pre-, post-, and the orgasmic stages of intercourse.

Terry Southern
(1924–1995) Writer, Actor, Producer

Her kisses left something to be desired—the rest of her.

 Author Unknown

130

ENJOYING SEX

Insightful Observations on
SEXUAL KNOWLEDGE

ABOUT A COLLEGE PAPER SHE WROTE ON MASTURBATION:
The research was remarkable!

  Claire Danes
(1979–) Actress

I sold my memoirs of my love life to Parker Brothers—they're going to make a game out of it.

  Woody Allen
(1935–) Director, Actor, Writer

Fewer college-age students today know the physiology of sex, and they depend much more on religious superstition and urban legend. They may know all about Britney Spears' belly button, but they wouldn't know the mechanics of a female orgasm if it popped out of their TV screens.

  Susie Bright
(1958–) Writer, Editor

GETTING STARTED
AVOIDING SEX
EXPERIENCING SEX
EXPERIMENTING
COMMON PROBLEMS
SEX AND SOCIETY

ENJOYING SEX

Insightful Observations on
THINKING DURING SEX

I don't think when I make love.

😎 **Brigitte Bardot**
(1934–) Actress, Sex Symbol

We think about sex obsessively except during the act, when our minds tend to wander.

😉 **Howard Nemerov**
(1920–) Poet

Many times while I was getting laid, in my head I was doing a business deal.

😉 **Arnold Schwarzenegger**
(1947–) Actor, Former Bodybuilder

THE GUIDE TO LAUGHING AT SEX

ENJOYING SEX

Insightful Observations on
REMEMBERING SEX

ANTHONY MICHAEL HALL: Did we, uhm?
HAVILAND MORRIS: Yeah, I'm pretty sure.
AMH: Excuse me, do you know if I enjoyed it? What am I— nuts? Of course I enjoyed it. What I meant was, did you?
HM: You know, I have this weird feeling I did.

 Anthony Michael Hall
and Haviland Morris
Sixteen Candles (1984)
written by John Hughes

People have come up with kinky sex because it's memorable.... When you do something kinky, it's like, yes, the mango sex. We'll always remember the mango sex. Try it, but try it with a sheet you can throw away, because there's nothing stickier than mango sex. It wasn't even that good, but we remember it. And that's the key—the remembering.

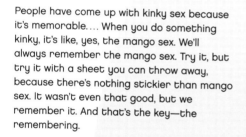 Beth Lapides
Comedian

You can't remember sex ... there is no memory of it in the brain, only the deduction that it happened and that time passed, leaving you with a silhouette that you want to fill in again.

 E.L. Doctorow
(1931–) Author

ENJOYING SEX

Insightful Observations on
SEX & LOVE

Sex is a momentary itch, love never lets you go.

 Kingsley Amis
(1922–1995) Novelist, Poet

Love is not the dying moan of a distant violin—it's the triumphant twang of a bedspring.

 S.J. Perelman
(1904–1979) Humorist, Writer

Love is an aphrodisiac and the main ingredient for lasting sex.

 Mort Katz
(1925–) Psychotherapist, Writer

For me love has to go very deep. Sex only has to go a few inches.

Stacey Nelkin
in *Bullets over Broadway* (1994) written by Woody Allen & Douglas McGrath

The difference between sex and love is that sex relieves tension and love causes it.

Woody Allen
(1935–) Director, Actor, Writer

Sex, a clever imitation of love. It has all the action but none of the plot.

 William Rotsler
(1926–1997) Author, Cartoonist

ENJOYING SEX

Insightful Observations on
SPIRITUAL SEX

When my house burned down, a friend sent out an e-mail suggesting people dedicate an orgasm to me. A lot of people did. The erotic prayer provided an amazing cushion. I felt so little pain.

Annie Sprinkle
(1954–) Porn Star,
Performance Artist,
Educator

Spiritual beings are also sexual. It's an aspect of being human. I believe posing for Playboy was definitely part of my life's path—I was meant to do it, maybe to set an example for other people, to help other people. It was my fate.

Tishara Cousino
(1978–) Model

Yoga is a very sexy way to work out. I think that anyone who pretends yoga's not about sex is just lying to you. And if they're saying, "It's very spiritual," well, it's not as if spirituality and sex aren't connected.

Beth Lapides
Comedian

There is a love that begins in the head and goes down to the heart, and grows slowly; but it lasts 'till death, and asks less than it gives. There is another love, that blots out wisdom, that is sweet with the sweetness of life and bitter with the bitterness of death, lasting for an hour, but it is worth having lived a whole life for that hour.

Ralph Iron
(1855–1920) South African
Writer

 = IDEALIST   = REALIST   = CYNIC

135

GETTING STARTED

AVOIDING SEX

EXPERIENCING SEX

EXPERIMENTING

COMMON PROBLEMS

SEX AND SOCIETY

ENJOYING SEX

Insightful Observations on
SEX & COMMUNICATION

When in doubt, fuck.

 Al Pacino
in *Scent of a Woman* (1992)
written by Bo Goldman

Sex is not the answer. Sex is the question. "Yes" is the answer.

Author Unknown

Sex is making a fool out of yourself.... That is why sex is so intimate. Making mistakes is one of the most revealing and intimate moments of sexual communication.

Jerry Rubin
(1938–1994) Journalist,
Therapist

The language of sex is yet to be invented. The language of the senses is yet to be explored.

Anais Nin
(1903–1977) French Author

You don't have to have a language in common with someone for sexual rapport. But it helps if the language you don't understand is Italian.

Madonna
(1958–) Singer, Songwriter,
Actress

Sex is hardly ever just about sex.

Shirley MacLaine
(1934–) Actress, Dancer,
Writer

I told my girlfriend that unless she expressed her feelings and told me what she liked, I wouldn't be able to please her, so she said, Get off me.

Garry Shandling
(1949–) Actor, Writer,
Comedian

THE GUIDE TO LAUGHING AT SEX

ENJOYING SEX

Insightful Observations on
EROGENOUS ZONES

One of the great breakthroughs in sex has been the discovery of all the new erogenous zones. Once it was thought there were only a handful. Now they are all over the place, with new ones being reported every day.

 Bruce Jay Friedman
(1930–) Author, Humorist

Erogenous zones are either everywhere or nowhere.

 Joseph Heller
(1923–1999) Writer

But women also have their problems. Thus making love to a girl for the first time can be like going into a dark room and fumbling for the electric switch. Only when a man has found it will the light come full on.

 Gerald Brenan
(1894–1987) Travel Writer, Novelist

What is my favorite romantic spot? You mean in the whole world or on somebody's body?

 Jackie Mason
(1934–) Comedian

The fact is there hasn't been a thrilling new erogenous zone discovered since de Sade.

 George Gilder
(1939–) Author, Educator, Researcher

GETTING STARTED

AVOIDING SEX

EXPERIENCING SEX

EXPERIMENTING

COMMON PROBLEMS

SEX AND SOCIETY

ENJOYING SEX

Insightful Observations on THE G-SPOT

I finally found my wife's G-Spot—a neighbor lady had it.

Jim Sherbert
Comedian

For women the best aphrodisiacs are words. The G-Spot is in the ears. He who looks for it below is wasting his time.

Isabel Allende
(1942–) Novelist

Somewhere over the rainbow,
Way up high:
There's a land that I heard of
Once in a lullaby.

E.Y. Harburg
(1896–1981) Songwriter; *The Wizard of Oz.*

In theory, trying to find your G-Spot is fairly simple. First, get naked. Then, lie down on your bed and put your finger in your vagina with your palm facing up (lubricating your finger will make this easier). Crook your finger and make a sort of 'come here big boy' motion. Near the front of your vagina, you may be able to feel a region of tissue, about the size of a penny, that feels different than the surrounding tissue. It may be slightly ridged, or feel a little bumpy or rough to the touch. That's your G-Spot.

Julia Starkey
Present Day Writer

138

ENJOYING SEX

Insightful Observations on
THE IMPORTANCE OF ORGASMS

At the moment of climax, there is a oneness with you and your husband and with God. When you come together, it's like when the church is brought up to meet Christ in the air.

 Anita Bryant
(1940–) Singer, Beauty Contestant, Moralist

MIRANDA: Orgasm? A major thing in a relationship?
CHARLOTTE: Yeah, but not the only thing. I mean, orgasms don't send you Valentine's day cards and they don't hold your hand in a sad movie.
CARRIE: Mine do.

 HBO's *Sex and the City*

An orgasm is a way of saying you enjoyed yourself, like complimenting the host on a wonderful spinach quiche.

 Helen Gurley Brown
(1922–) Author, Editor

A man must be potent and orgasmic to ensure the future of the race. A woman only needs to be available.

 Masters & Johnson
William Masters (1915–2001), a gynecologist, teamed with Virginia Johnson (1925–) as Authors and Human Sexuality Researchers.

The orgasm has replaced the Cross as the focus of longing and the image of fulfillment.

 Malcolm Muggeridge
(1903–1990) Journalist, Sage

ENJOYING SEX

Insightful Observations on FAKING ORGASMS

I may not be a great actress but I've become the greatest at screen orgasms. Ten seconds of heavy breathing, roll your head from side to side, simulate a slight asthma attack, and die a little.

 Candice Bergen
(1946–) Actress

Even if it wasn't good, she could fake it the best.

 Keanu Reeves
(1964–) Actor; **on his fantasy to have sex with Meryl Streep**

You're down by five with thirty seconds left in the game. This is going to be amazing. You're screaming at the top of your lungs. The quarterback sends a long, smooth pass to the end zone. Your star receiver's open, the ball is sailing straight toward him; he waits in the end zone for his moment of glory. The ball's flight is interrupted as it grazes his fingertips and falls to the ground. He's missed it. You stop screaming. You feign being a good sport, but deep down, you're disappointed. No matter how loud, how convincingly you cheered, you didn't get yours. This is exactly what faking an orgasm feels like.

 Natalie Krinsky
Yale Univeristy Sex Columnist

Women might be able to fake orgasms. But men can fake whole relationships.

 Sharon Stone
(1958–) Actress

140

ENJOYING SEX

Insightful Observations on PACING SEX

Fondle the woman in your life once for every thousand times you play with your private parts. That should be enough.

 Barbara Graham
(1923–1955) Writer

Yes, that's correct—20,000 different ladies. At my age that equals out to having sex with 1.2 women everyday, everyday since I was 15.

 Wilt Chamberlain
(1936–1999) Basketball Player

Sex after children slows down. Every three months now we have sex. Every time I have sex, the next day I pay my quarterly taxes. Unless it's oral sex—then I renew driver's license.

 Ray Romano
(1957–) Actor, Comedian

My wife had cut our lovemaking down to once a month, but I know two guys she's cut out entirely.

 Rodney Dangerfield
(1921–) Actor, Comedian

ENJOYING SEX

Insightful Observations on
DELAYED GRATIFICATION

Anything worth doing well is worth doing slowly.

 Gypsy Rose Lee
(1914–1970) Dancer,
Entertainer, Author

First, we'll have an orgy and then we'll go see Tony Bennett.

 Elliott Gould
in *Bob & Carol & Ted & Alice*
(1969) written by Paul
Mazursky & Larry Tucker

I like a man that takes his time.

 Mae West
(1892–1980) Actress, Writer

For flavor, instant sex will never supersede the stuff you have to peel and cook.

 Quentin Crisp
(1908–1999) Writer

The longer they wait, the better they like it.

 Marlene Dietrich
(1901–1992) German Actress

THE GUIDE TO LAUGHING AT SEX

ENJOYING SEX

Insightful Observations on
PROMISCUOUS MEN

The chief occupation of my life has been to cultivate the pleasures of the senses. Feeling myself born for the fair sex, I have always loved it, and have been loved in return as often as possible.

Casanova
(1725–1798) Italian Adventurer; Seducer

A promiscuous person is usually someone who is getting more sex than you are.

Victor Lownes
Former "Head" of *Playboy* in the U.K.

It ain't sex that's troublesome, it's staying up all night looking for it.

Casey Stengel
(1891–1975) Baseball Player; Manager

Who's Virginia?

Rose Kennedy
(1890–1995) Mother of Kennedy Politicians; **when told her daughter-in-law Joan lived in Boston and her son Ted lived in Virginia**

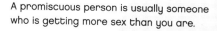

= IDEALIST   = REALIST   = CYNIC

143

ENJOYING SEX

Insightful Observations on
PROMISCUOUS WOMEN

What part of a woman is her 'now'? I only ask because I hear that everybody's kissing her now.

 Author Unknown

Who cares what you are—just enjoy it!

Kim Cattrall
in HBO's *Sex and the City*

I'm saving the bass player for Omaha.

Janis Joplin
(1943–1970) American Rock Singer

I don't think I'm gay. I don't think I'm straight. I think I'm just slutty. Where's my parade?

Margaret Cho
(1968–) Comedian, Actress

I feel like a million tonight—but one at a time.

Mae West
(1892–1980) Actress, Writer

You were born with your legs apart. They'll send you to the grave in a Y-shaped coffin.

Joe Orton
(1933–1967) British Dramatist

You know, she speaks eighteen languages. And she can't say `No' in any of them

Dorothy Parker
(1893–1967) Writer

THE GUIDE TO LAUGHING AT SEX

ENJOYING SEX

Insightful Observations on
DOUBLE STANDARD

Women's virtue is man's greatest invention.

 Cornelia Otis Skinner
(1901–1979) Stage Actress

We still have these double standards where the emphasis is all on the male's sexual appetites—that it's OK for him to collect as many scalps as he can before he settles down and pays the price. If a woman displays the same attitude, all the epithets that exist in the English language are laid at her door, and with extraordinary bitterness.

Glenda Jackson
(1936–) Actress, Politician

A man can sleep around, no questions asked, but if a woman makes nineteen or twenty mistakes, she's a tramp.

 Joan Rivers
(1933–) Actress, Comedian

Indeed you could say as a general rule: men get laid and women get screwed.

 Quentin Crisp
(1908–1999) Writer

Step Four:

EXPERIM

ENTING

Fantasy

Kinky Sex

Alternative Sex

GETTING STARTED

AVOIDING SEX

EXPERIENCING SEX

EXPERIMENTING

COMMON PROBLEMS

SEX AND SOCIETY

FANTASY

Insightful Observations on
EXPERIMENTING WITH SEX

Normal love isn't interesting. I assure you that it's incredibly boring.

 Roman Polanski
(1933–) Director, Actor

There is no norm in sex. Norm is the name of a guy who lives in Brooklyn.

 Dr. Alex Comfort
(1920–2000) British Writer, Sexologist

We tried it [sex] twice and it worked both times.

 Robert Benchley
(1889–1945) Writer, Humorist, Actor

I caused my husband's heart attack. In the middle of lovemaking I took the paper bag off my head. He dropped the Polaroid and keeled over and so did the hooker. It would have taken me half an hour to untie myself and call the paramedics, but fortunately the Great Dane could dial.

☺ **Joan Rivers**
(1933–) Actress, Comedian

FANTASY

Insightful Observations on
SEX & FANTASY

When turkeys mate, they think of swans.

 Johnny Carson
(1925–) Comedian, Talk Show Host

I believe that the human imagination never invented anything that was not true, in this world or any other.

Gerard de Nerval
(1808–1855) Poet

Sex is not imaginary, but it is not quite real either.

Mason Cooley
(1927–) Aphorist

Fantasy love is much better than reality love. Never doing it is very exciting. The most exciting attractions are between two opposites that never meet.

Andy Warhol
(1928–1987) Pop Artist, Filmmaker

Sick and perverted always appeals to me.

Madonna
(1958–)Singer, Songwriter, Actress

Man's Desires are limited by his Perceptions; none can desire what he has not perceived.

William Blake
(1757–1827) British Poet

😃 = IDEALIST   😊 = REALIST   🙂 = CYNIC

149

FANTASY

Insightful Observations on
MALE SEX FANTASY

I don't think anyone conceives of sex the way I do: surrealistic and rich with humor.

 Woody Allen
(1935–) Director, Actor, Writer

Marilyn Monroe was a masturbation-fantasy of bellboys; Grace Kelly of bank executives.

 James Dickey
(1923–1997) Poet, Writer

Were it not for imagination, sir, a man would be as happy in the arms of a chambermaid as of a duchess.

Dr. Samuel Johnson
(1709–1784) Lexicographer, Critic, Poet

Why fuck the girl in the skirt if you can fuck the girl in the ad for the skirt?

 Nick Waxler
Modelizer on HBO's *Sex and the City*

Sometimes it's Britney Spears, and sometimes it's Carrie Fisher. I can't tell if I have a Lolita Complex or an Oedipus Complex.

 Ben Affleck
(1972–) Actor, Writer

FANTASY

Insightful Observations on
FEMALE
SEX FANTASY

In my sex fantasy, nobody ever loves me for my mind.

😁 **Nora Ephron**
(1941–) Writer, Director

My ultimate fantasy is to entice a man to my bedroom, put a gun to his head and say, "Make babies or die."

😁 **Ruby Wax**
(1953-) Actress, Comedian, Writer

You fantasize about a man with a Park Avenue apartment and a nice big stock portfolio.... For me, it's a fireman with a nice big hose.

😉 **Kim Cattrall**
in HBO's *Sex and the City*

BILLY CRYSTAL: That's it? A faceless guy rips off your clothes and that's the sex fantasy you've been having since you were twelve. Exactly the same?
MEG RYAN: Well, sometimes I vary it a little.
BC: Which part?
MR: What I'm wearing.

😉 ***When Harry Met Sally***
(1989) written by Nora Ephron

My wife said her wildest sexual fantasy would be if I got my own apartment.

🙂 **Rodney Dangerfield**
(1921–) Actor, Comedian

After sex, the man dies.

🙂 **Emily Levine**
Comedian, Writer; **on her sexual fantasies**

FANTASY

Insightful Observations on
CELEBRITY FANTASY

I want to be reincarnated as Warren Beatty's fingertips.

 Woody Allen
(1935–) Director, Actor, Writer

I used to move in with people and fuck them because I thought they'd give me their powers. And they did.

 Courtney Love
(1965–) Singer, Actress

Do we have sex? Yes, yes, yes.

 Lisa Marie Presley
(1968–) Singer; Daughter of Elvis Presley; **on her marriage to Michael Jackson**

No head, no backstage pass.

 David Allen Coe
(1939–) Singer, Songwriter, Musician, Actor; **printed on his roadcrew's T-shirts**

THE GUIDE TO LAUGHING AT SEX

FANTASY

Insightful Observations on
HOW FAR SHOULD I GO?

Try everything once except incest and folk dancing.

Sir Thomas Beecham
(1879–1961) Conductor, Impresario

The only unnatural sex act is that which you cannot perform.

Alfred Kinsey
(1894–1956) Entomologist, Sexuality Researcher

Take naked pictures … share your fantasies … be your own 900 number.

Yvonne Fulbright
New York University Sex Columnist

There are two guidelines in good sex: don't do anything you really don't enjoy, and find out your partner's needs and don't balk if you can help it.

Dr. Alex Comfort
(1920–2000) British Writer, Sexologist

I've tried everything but coprophagia and necrophillia, and I like kissing best.

John Waters
(1946–) Actor, Writer

Since time began nobody has been able to copulate while asleep. Even if it were possible it would be impolite.

Alan Sherman
(1924–1973) Writer, Producer

INSIGHTFUL OBSERVATIONS TO SHARE

FANTASY

Insightful Observations on ROLE PLAYING

Elderly husband says to his wife as she prepares to enter the living room: "Ready, Harold? You're the wicked troll and I'm the garden fairy, and you're very angry because you don't want me passing over your bridge on my way to Grandma's house!"

 George Booth
Present Day Cartoonist in the *New Yorker*

Sometimes I sing and dance around the house in my underwear. Doesn't make me Madonna. Never will.

 Joan Cusack
in *Working Girl* (1988) written by Kevin Wade

Nothing is either all masculine or all feminine except having sex.

 Marlo Thomas
(1938–) Actress, Writer

Men are boring to women because there's only about twelve types of us and they know all the keys. And they're bored by the fact we never escape our types.

 Jack Nicholson
(1937–) Actor, ScreenWriter, Producer, Director

I've made so many movies playing a hooker that they don't pay me in the regular way anymore. They leave it on the dresser.

 Shirley MacLaine
(1934–) Actress, Dancer, Writer

During sex I fantasize that I'm someone else.

 Richard Lewis
(1947–) Comedian, Actor

154

FANTASY

Insightful Observations on
UNIFORMS

Eventually, all men come out of the bathroom dressed as a majorette.

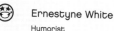 **Ernestyne White**
Humorist

My husband is German; every night I get dressed up like Poland and he invades me.

😁 **Bette Midler**
(1944–) Actress, Singer, Comedian

Men frequently fantasize fucking a nun, a nurse, or indeed a policewoman, and when I had my house, in New York, I had regular johns who would ask for girls in these various disguises.

😉 **Xaviera Hollander**
(1943–) Madam, Writer

The Duke returned from the wars today and did pleasure me in his top-boots.

😉 **Sarah, Duchess of Marlborough**
(1660– 1744) Wife of John Churchill, 1st Duke of Marlborough.

GETTING STARTED

AVOIDING SEX

EXPERIENCING SEX

EXPERIMENTING

COMMON PROBLEMS

SEX AND SOCIETY

FANTASY

Insightful Observations on BAD GIRLS

Give me a couple of drinks and I'll be the bitch.

 Sir Elton John
(1947–) Rock Singer, Musician

When I'm good, I'm very good; when I'm bad, I'm better.

Mae West
(1892–1980) Actress, Writer

Good girls go to heaven, bad girls go everywhere.

Helen Gurley Brown
(1922–) Author, Editor

There was a little girl, Who had a little curl Right in the middle of her forehead, When she was good she was very very good And when she was bad she was very very popular.

Max Miller
(1895–1963) British Music-Hall Comedian

I may be good for nothing, but I'm never bad for nothing.

Mae West
(1892–1980) Actress, Writer

A pessimist is a man who thinks all women are bad; an optimist is one who hopes they are.

Chauncey M. Depew
(1834–1928) Businessman, Public Official

THE GUIDE TO LAUGHING AT SEX

FANTASY

Insightful Observations on PERVERSIONS

Maybe I'll make a Mary Poppins movie and shove the umbrella up my ass.

 Marilyn Chambers
(1952–) 70's porn star

Sex is the metaphor that I use, but for me, it's about love. It's about tolerance, acceptance and saying, "Look, everybody has different needs and wants and preferences and desires and fantasies. And we should not damn somebody because it's different than ours."

 Madonna
(1958–) Singer; Songwriter; Actress

One half of the world cannot understand the pleasures of the other.

 Jane Austen
(1775–1817) British Novelist

It is very disturbing indeed when you can't think of any new perversions that you would like to practice.

 James Dickey
(1923–1997) Poet, Writer

Please get over the notion that your particular "thing" is something that only the deepest, saddest, the most nobly tortured can know. It ain't. It's just one kind of sex— that's all. And, in my opinion, the universe turns regardless.

 Lorraine Hansberry
(1930–1965) Dramatist

I think extreme heterosexuality is a perversion.

 Margaret Mead
(1901–1978) Anthropologist

 = IDEALIST   = REALIST   = CYNIC

157

GETTING STARTED

AVOIDING SEX

EXPERIENCING SEX

EXPERIMENTING

COMMON PROBLEMS

SEX AND SOCIETY

KINKY SEX

Insightful Observations on VOYEURS

I like to watch.

Peter Sellers
to Shirley MacLaine, in
Being There (1979) written by
Jerzy Kosinski; **Sellers
meant 'television,' MacLain
was thinking 'sex'**

I just wanted to see what it looked like in the spotlight.

Jim Morrison
(1943–1971) Singer,
Songwriter; **on why he
exposed himself on stage**

When I find a woman attractive, I have nothing at all to say. I simply watch her smile.

Antoine de Saint-Exupery
(1900–1944) French Aviator,
Writer

I called my book Sex because it was a very provocative title and I knew people would want to buy it and look at the pictures and yet they denounce it at the same time, so I thought, that's a statement of our society in itself.

Madonna
(1958–) Singer, Songwriter,
Actress

KINKY SEX

Insightful Observations on EXHIBITIONISTS

I'm just looking for that moment to drop my Jedi knickers and pull out my real light saber.

😵 **Ewan McGregor**
(1971–) Actor

I'm in one of those stirrup tables that gynecologists have when they spread your legs and look deep inside of you. But the table is in the middle of the ring, in Madison Square Garden, and it's mounted on a revolving platform. Thousands of men have paid fifty or one hundred dollars each for tickets, and the ushers are selling binoculars so they can get a better view.

😵 **Nancy Friday**
(1937–) Writer, Psychologist

If you see a man playing with his penis in front of you, you don't think it's a cop.

😉 **George Michael**
(1964–) Singer, Songwriter; **on the cop that busted him**

There are certain people who should know what you look like naked. I just don't think your high school algebra teacher is one of them.

😏 **Julia Roberts**
(1969–) Actress, **on appearing naked in a film**

Twelve percent of women have posed nude for a photo.

😊 **Glamour Magazine Poll**

It's impolite to have sex anywhere that is visable to other people who aren't having sex.

🙂 **Jenny Eclair**
(1960–) British Actress, Writer

GETTING STARTED

AVOIDING SEX

EXPERIENCING SEX

EXPERIMENTING

COMMON PROBLEMS

SEX AND SOCIETY

KINKY SEX

Insightful Observations on
BEING NAUGHTY

If everything was coated with a seal of approval, some of the fun would go out of it. Let's get away with something. Degrade me, baby.

 Sallie Tisdale
(1957–) Author, Editor

I'd like to try in your house sometime. The idea of doing it in my sister's bed gives me a perverse thrill.

Laura San Giacomo
in Sex, Lies & Videotape
(1989) written by Steven Soderberg

I was naughty, I wasn't bad. Bad is hurting people. Naughty is being amusing.

Sydney Biddle Barrows
(1952–) Mayflower Madam

Catholic guilt is definitely a weird aphrodisiac. Once you start getting turned on, you know, being bad, and now you're outside the law and outside the blessings of God. You're in the devil's camp, and you might as well just go all the way. Sex for a lot of us is like being thrown off a cliff.

Lisa Carver
(1969–) Writer

She knew, even though she was too young to know the reason, that indiscriminate desire and unselective sex were possible only to those who regarded sex and themselves as evil.

Ayn Rand
(1905–1982) Novelist

As pure as the driven slush.

 Tallulah Bankhead
(1903– 1968) Actress

THE GUIDE TO LAUGHING AT SEX

KINKY SEX

Insightful Observations on EVIL SEX

What I say is that the supreme and singular joy of making love resides in the certainty of doing evil.

 Charles Baudelaire
(1821–1867) Symbolist Poet

There is a little bit of vampire instinct in every woman.

Theda Bara
(1890–1955) Silent Film Star

If a man has a right to find God in his own way, he has a right to go to the Devil in his own way also.

Hugh Hefner
(1926–) Founder of *Playboy*

I make it a rule never to get involved with possessed people. [KISS] Actually, it's more of a guideline than a rule.

Bill Murray
to Sigourney Weaver in
Ghostbusters (1984) written
by Dan Aykroyd & Harold
Ramis

You cannot separate young limbs and lechery.

William Shakespeare
(1564–1616) Playwright, Poet

If a woman hasn't got a tiny streak of the harlot in her, she's a dry stick.

 D.H. Lawrence
(1885–1930) Novelist, Poet,
Essayist

INSIGHTFUL OBSERVATIONS TO SHARE

GETTING STARTED
AVOIDING SEX
EXPERIENCING SEX
EXPERIMENTING
COMMON PROBLEMS
SEX AND SOCIETY

KINKY SEX

Insightful Observations on
KINKY SEX

I'm aroused by the idea of a woman making love to me while either a man or another woman watches. Is that kinky?

Madonna
(1958–) Singer, Songwriter, Actress

I'm not kinky, but occasionally I like to put on a robe and stand in front of a tennis ball machine.

Garry Shandling
(1949–) Actor, Writer, Comedian

I'd rather laugh in bed than do it.... If I went to a lady of the night, I'd probably pay her to tell me jokes. Would that be perverted?

Billy Joel
(1949–) Singer, Songwriter

Kinky sex involves the use of duck feathers. Perverted sex involves the whole duck.

Lewis Grizzard
(1947–) Southern Humorist

He had a red dress on, and a black feather boa around his neck. And Hoover had a Bible. He wanted one of the boys to read from the Bible. And he read ... and the other boy played with him, wearing the rubber gloves.

Susan Rosenstiel
Fourth Wife of reputed mob boss, Lewis Rosenstiel; quoted in *Official and Confidential: The Secret Life of J. Edgar Hoover* written by Anthony Summers

KINKY SEX

Insightful Observations on
DIRTY SEX

Is sex dirty? Only if it's done right.

 Woody Allen
(1935–) Director, Actor, Writer

Sex touches the heavens only when it simultaneously touches the gutter and the mud.

George Jean Nathan
(1882–1958) Editor, Critic

I thank God I was raised Catholic, so sex will always be dirty.

John Waters
(1946–) Actor, Writer

The spirit is most often free when the body is satiated with pleasure; indeed, sometimes the stars shine more brightly seen from the gutter than from the hilltop.

 W. Somerset Maugham
(1874–1965) Writer

When grown-ups do it, it's kind of dirty—that's because there is no one to punish them.

Tuesday Weld
(1943–) Actress

It was never dirty to me. After all, God gave us the equipment and the opportunity. There's that old saying, "If God had meant for us to fly, he'd have given us wings." Well, look what he did give us.

 Dolly Parton
(1946–) Singer, Songwriter, Actress

KINKY SEX

Insightful Observations on
DOMINANT WOMEN

Yes ... I have big balls ... and I'm not afraid to use them.

 Mistress Ren
Professional Dominatrix

A riding crop and a blindfold doesn't make it BDSM. There is a big difference between being kinky and being in the scene. It's not a sexual thing to me, it's a very spiritual thing.

 DominaBlue
Professional Dominatrix

I love men. I think that's confusing to people. Like how could you be a dominatrix and beat men up ... and like men. The thing is, exactly the opposite is true: if you don't like men, you'll never survive in this business.

 Mistress Natasha
Professional Dominatrix

There are two kinds of women: those who want power in the world, and those who want power in bed.

 Jacqueline Kennedy Onassis
(1929–1994) Former First Lady, Editor

Straight men need to be emasculated. I'm sorry. They all need to be slapped around. Women have been kept down for too long.

 Madonna
(1958–) Singer, Songwriter, Actress

164

KINKY SEX

Insightful Observations on SPANKING

Coffee without caffeine is like sex without spanking.

Jeremy Piven
as Trevor "Cupid" Hale in the TV sitcom *Cupid*, written by Michael Green & Elle Triedman

You don't appreciate a lot of stuff in school until you get older. Little things like being spanked everyday by a middle-aged woman: Stuff you pay good money for in later life.

Emo Philips
Present Day Comedian

Spanking chic dominates the marketplace these days. Barnes and Noble stocks up for Valentine's Day with Patricia Payne's Sex Tips from a Dominatrix. Inept partners bungle with hairbrushes on Ally McBeal. Vodka peddlers shackle their bottles for that Absolute Sadist look. At S&M supper clubs, it's duck for dinner and discipline for dessert. Spanking is hip, and—as with 1970's porno chic, where "nice" couples flocked to see Deep Throat—middle-class American consumers are eating it up.

Chris Daley
Writer

Don't do that again. For me, it isn't erotic.

Christopher Eigeman
to Isabel Gillies in *Metropolitan* (1990) written by Whit Stillman

= IDEALIST   = REALIST   = CYNIC

KINKY SEX

Insightful Observations on
BONDAGE

Get in good physical condition before submitting to bondage. You should be fit to be tied.

Robert Byrne
(1930–) Author, Humorist

ON THE MYSTERIOUS DISAPPEARANCE OF HANDCUFFS FROM RESTRAINT KITS: Clearly our crews are so professional, they practice restraint procedures at home.

A British Airways Spokeswoman

Whenever I call upon a woman, I never fail to take with me a little whip.

Friedrich Nietzsche
(1844–1900) German Philosopher

Chains required, whips optional.

California Highway Sign

More extreme forms of bondage involve homes in the suburbs, station wagons, household food budgets, and Little League coaching activities and are too alarming and repulsive to discuss in print.

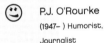
P.J. O'Rourke
(1947–) Humorist, Journalist

THE GUIDE TO LAUGHING AT SEX

KINKY SEX

Insightful Observations on INFLICTING PAIN

The two best teachers are love and pain.

😆 **Marcia Gay Harden**
in *The Education of Max Bixford* TV series

Pleasure does not exist without pain. Pain and pleasure are the same emotion.

😆 **Marquis de Sade**
(1740–1814) French Author

VALERIA GOLINO: We were only hurting each other.
CARY ELWES: I thought that's the way you wanted it.

😉 *Hot Shots!*
(1991) written by Jim Abrahams & Pat Proft

I'm all for bringing back the birch, but only between consenting adults.

😉 **Gore Vidal**
(1925–) Novelist, Playwright, Essayist

Look, if you want to torture me, spank me, lick me, do it. But if this poetry shit continues, just shoot me now please.

🙂 **Lori Petty**
in *Tank Girl* (1995) written by Tedi Sarafian

GETTING STARTED

AVOIDING SEX

EXPERIENCING SEX

EXPERIMENTING

COMMON PROBLEMS

SEX AND SOCIETY

KINKY SEX

Insightful Observations on
ENJOYING PAIN

Ouch! That felt good!

 Karen Elizabeth Gordon
Author, Illustrator

Sticks and stones may break my bones but whips and chains excite me.

 Author Unknown

ALGOPHIA, sexual arousal through pain is surprisingly common. In 1953 the Kinsey report said that 50% of people were aroused after being bitten. One source said the 17% of the U.S. population indulges in some sort of sadomasochistic activity.

 Sex, A Users Guide
by Stephen Arnott

No pleasure without pain.

 Proverb
Attributed to Budda, Plato & Socrates

When a masochist brings someone home and puts the moves on her, does he say, "Excuse me a moment, I'm going to slip into something uncomfortable?"

 George Carlin
(1938–) Comedian, Actor, Writer

THE GUIDE TO LAUGHING AT SEX

KINKY SEX

Insightful Observations on SUBMISSION

If you can't beat 'em ... let them beat you.

 Mistress Xaveness

When you're slapped, you'll take it and like it.

 Humphrey Bogart
to Peter Lorre in *The Maltese Falcon* (1941) written by John Huston, novel by Dashiell Hammett

Women, by nature, want to be dominated.

 Jayne Mansfield
(1933–1967) Actress

Submission without domination is when you keep doing what he wants even after he keeps insisting he doesn't want it. Domination without submission is when he keeps telling you to do something and you keep telling him to fuck off.

 Author Unknown

You have to accept the fact that part of the sizzle of sex comes from the danger of sex. That you can be overpowered.

 Camille Paglia
(1947–) Author, Critic, Educator

KINKY SEX

Insightful Observations on
BEING SUBMISSIVE

At times, it is strangely sedative to know the extent of your own powerlessness

 Erica Jong
(1942–) Writer, Poet

I do not want to be the leader. I refuse to be the leader. I want to live darkly and richly in my femaleness. I want a man lying over me, always over me. His will, his pleasure, his desire, his life, his work, his sexuality the touchstone, the command, my pivot. I don't mind working, holding my ground intellectually, artistically; but as a woman, oh, God, as a woman I want to be dominated. I don't mind being told to stand on my own feet, not to cling all that I am capable of doing but I am going to be pursued, fucked, possessed by the will of a male at his time, his bidding.

Anaïs Nin
(1903–1977) Writer

ALAN ALDA: No.
JANE FONDA: No what?
ALAN ALDA: No sir.

 California Suite
(1978) written by Neil Simon

Even though I got liberated, it's still very complicated. I say to men, "Okay, pretend you're a burglar and you've broken in here and you throw me down on the bed and make me suck your cock!" And they're horrified. It goes against all they've recently been taught. "No, no, it would degrade you!" Exactly. Degrade me when I ask you to.

 Lisa Palac
(1963–) Writer, Editor

170

KINKY SEX

Insightful Observations on
THREE-WAY SEX

Do Siamese twins count as one or two?

 Howard Stern
(1954–) Radio Personality

The biggest problem with a ménage à trois is that when it's all over and you open your eyes, they're still there. And you have to say something nice. And you wonder if you're a pervert.

 Lisa Carver
(1969–) Writer

Women are really not that exacting. They only desire one thing in bed. Take off your socks. And by the way—they're never going to invite their best girlfriend over for a threesome, so you can stop asking.

 Dennis Miller
(1953–) Actor, Comedian

Three ways are so physically and emotionally exhausting because they do not occur in nature. You never see a gazelle three-way on a National Geographic special. Because they know better. Only man is fool enough to spit in the eye of God.... God does not like three-way.

 Lisa Carver
(1969–) Writer

KINKY SEX

Insightful Observations on
ORGIES

Sex between a man and a woman can be wonderful—provided you get between the right man and the right woman.

 Woody Allen
(1935–) Director, Actor, Writer

Home is heaven and orgies are vile
But you need an orgy, once in a while.

Ogden Nash
(1902–1971) Poet

Once: a Philosopher; twice: a pervert!

Voltaire
(1694–1778) French Writer, Philosopher; **turning down an invitation to an orgy, having attended one the previous night**

You get a better class of person at orgies, because people have to keep in trim more. There is an awful lot of going round holding in your stomach, you know. Everybody is very polite to each other. The conversation isn't very good but you can't have everything.

Gore Vidal
(1925–) Novelist, Playwright, Essayist

If God had meant us to have group sex, he'd have given us more organs.

Malcolm Bradbury
(1932–2000) Writer, Critic

THE GUIDE TO LAUGHING AT SEX

KINKY SEX

Insightful Observations on
SWINGERS

Si Non Oscillas Noli Tintinnare. (If you don't swing, don't ring.)

Brass Plaque
on the door of the Playboy Mansion

Chasing the naughty couples down the grassgreen gooseberried double bed of the wood.

Dylan Thomas
(1914–1953) Welsh Poet

If you've been around at all you know that female teachers rank among the world's greatest swingers. Put a knowledgeable guy in a bar loaded with women of different backgrounds and he'll head for the teacher. He knows.

Trudy Baker & Rachel Jones
Authors; *Coffee Tea or Me*

Non-spontaneous sex is creepy, boring, and passe. Practitioners of sport call themselves swingers. (I ask you.) Swingers are all from the suburbs and consequently brain-addled by car pools, shopping malls, and welcome wagons. Swinger men affect furtive eyes and oozing glutinous voices. Swinger women wear complicated hairdos and sheepish expressions.

Cynthia Heimel
Present Day Writer; Humorist

There are women whose infidelities are the only link they still have with their husbands.

Sacha Guitry
(1885–1957) French Playwrite, Actor

 = IDEALIST   = REALIST   😊 = CYNIC

173

GETTING STARTED

AVOIDING SEX

EXPERIENCING SEX

EXPERIMENTING

COMMON PROBLEMS

SEX AND SOCIETY

KINKY SEX

Insightful Observations on FETISHES

Face it. After Marv Albert, no fetish is really shocking.

 Maxim Magazine

Nothing risque, nothing gained.

 Alexander Woollcott
(1887–1943) Journalist

My favorite fetish is wrestling. Men show up, put on their wrestling outfits and I scissor kick them or hold them down. No sex is involved and I get $250 an hour for that service. It's quite popular. Plus, I usually get to win.

 Joya
6' 1" 170llb, Prostitute

Prof. Higgins was right—men wish that woman's sexuality was like theirs, which it isn't. Male sexuality is far brisker and more automatic. Your clothes, breasts, odor, etc., aren't what he loves instead of you—they are simply the things he needs in order to set sex in motion to express love. Women find this hard to understand.

Dr. Alex Comfort
(1920–2000) British Writer, Sexologist

My own belief is that there is hardly anyone whose sexual life, if it were broadcast, would not fill the world at large with surprise and horror.

W. Somerset Maugham
(1874–1965) Writer

The mind of the person who's interested in legs and feet is very different from the person who's interested in breasts. Breast men tend to be aggressive, outgoing, athletic—whereas people who like the lower body tend to be frightened, introverted. It all has to do with being down on the floor when you're a scared little child and looking up at that big tower of mommy. What's down there—the feet and the legs, that's where security is.

Dian Hanson
Fetish Magazine Editor for *Big Butt, Outlaw Biker, Tight, Leg Show & Juggs*

174

KINKY SEX

Insightful Observations on
FOOT FETISHES

A pretty foot is one of the greatest gifts of nature.... Please send me your last pair of shoes, already worn out in dancing, so I can have something of yours to press against my heart.

😵 **Johann Wolfgang Goethe**
(1749–1832) Dramatist, Novelist, Scientist

Very few people will suck toes. They think it is foot fetishism. People don't want to suck toes and they don't want to talk about life. Men always expect you to suck them but they don't suck.

😊 **Lily Tomlin**
(1939–) Comedian, Actress

Quite by accident I recently hit on what I hope is the ultimate secret of foot fetishism. In the foot it has become permissible to worship the long last and ardently longed for woman's penis of the primordial age of infancy. Evidently some people search as passionatley for this precious object as the pious English do for the lost ten tribes of Israel.

😉 **Sigmund Freud**
(1856–1939) Doctor, Founder of Psychoanalysis; **in a letter to Carl Jung (1909)**

There is no unhappier creature on earth than the fetishist who yearns for a woman's shoe and has to embrace the whole woman.

😐 **Karl Kraus**
(1874–1936) Austrian Writer

KINKY SEX

Insightful Observations on
PIERCING

One of my students had a piercing through her labia. And she told me about how when you ride on a motorcycle, the little bead on the ring acts like a vibrator. Her story turned me on so I did it. I got two.

Kathy Acker
(1947–1999) Writer,
Professor

A lovely ring that I wear in a very special place. One of my [vaginal] lips … it's pierced, and he thought that this part of my body had made a lot of money and fame and it deserved a present.

Marilyn Chambers
(1952–) 70's Porn Star; **on a gift given to her by Sammy Davis Jr.**

Read the instructions that come with your cock ring. They're certainly more entertaining than the ones for your VCR.

Rachael Klein
University of California,
Berkley Sex Columnist

I just had a penis piercing done, but I've received differing opinions about whether I'm going to have trouble with airport metal detectors. What's scoop?

H.J. of St. Louis, Missouri
in a letter to *Playboy*

A friend of mine got her clitoral hood pierced. I think that's disgusting. I would never do that. I'd get a clip-on.

Sarah Silverman
Comedian, Writer

THE GUIDE TO LAUGHING AT SEX

ALTERNATIVE SEX

Insightful Observations on SEX TOYS

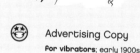

That delicious, thrilling, health-restoring sensation called vibration.... It makes you fairly tingle with the joy of living.

😵 **Advertising Copy**
For vibrators; early 1900s

A plastic lady is no substitute. Plastic squeaks.

😊 **Dudley Moore**
(1935–2002) Actor, Comedian, Writer, Musician

If you use the electric vibrator near water, you will come and go at the same time.

😉 **Louise Sammons**
Humorist

There are a number of mechanical devices which increase sexual arousal, particularly in women. Chief among them is the Mercedes-Benz convertible.

😏 **P.J. O'Rourke**
(1947–) Humorist, Journalist

I am through with men.... I just want to be left alone with my vibrator. Yet another example of men being replaced by their machines.

🙂 **Lisa Alther**
(1944–) Writer

CARRIE: I'm not going to replace a man with some battery-operated device.
MIRANDA: You haven't met "The Rabbit."
SAMANTHA: Oh come one, if you're going to get a vibrator, at least get one called "The Horse."

🙂 **Sarah Jessica Parker, Cynthia Nixon & Kim Cattrall**
in HBO's *Sex and the City*

INSIGHTFUL OBSERVATIONS TO SHARE

ALTERNATIVE SEX

Insightful Observations on
CROSS DRESSING

All my life I wanted to look like Liz Taylor. Now I find that Liz Taylor is beginning to look like me.

Divine
(1945–1988) Transvestite Actor

You must understand that this is not a woman's dress I'm wearing. It's a man's dress.

David Bowie
(1947–) Rock singer; on wearing a dress while performing

I never wear designer things, but I'm a great supporter of women's fashion. I like to actually wear women's fashion.

Hugh Grant
(1960–) Actor

I do like making boys wear my high heels and earrings. But not my panties, because that's not going to look very pretty.

Elizabeth Hurley
(1965–) Actress

People ask, "Why do you dress like a woman?" I don't dress like a woman. I dress like a drag queen."

RuPaul
(1960–) Drag Queen, Performer

178

ALTERNATIVE SEX

Insightful Observations on
PLACES & SEX

Hooray! Hooray! The first of May! Outdoor screwing begins today!

 Folk Rhyme

COUPLE TALKING AS THEY MAKE LOVE ON THE FLOOR OF A BOOKSTORE: "This never could have happened at www.amazon.com."

 William Hamilton
Present Day Cartoonist in the *New Yorker*

You can't make love on wet sand ... it just gets into everything.

Jayne Mansfield
in *Will Success Spoil Rock Hunter?* (1957) written by Frank Tashlin, play by George Axelrod

The requirements of romantic love are difficult to satisfy in the trunk of a Dodge Dart.

 Lisa Alther
(1944–) Writer

Beware of men on airplanes. The minute a man reaches thirty thousand feet, he immediately becomes consumed by distasteful sexual fantasies which involve doing uncomfortable things in those tiny toilets. These men should not be encouraged, their fantasies are sadly low rent and unimaginative.... Unless, of course, he's a pilot.

 Cynthia Heimel
Present Day Writer, Humorist

Please. This isn't the Gap.

 Salesmen
to Carrie and Sam, making out in a Banana Republic dressing room in HBO's *Sex and the City*

GETTING STARTED

AVOIDING SEX

EXPERIENCING SEX

EXPERIMENTING

COMMON PROBLEMS

SEX AND SOCIETY

ALTERNATIVE SEX

Insightful Observations on
ONLINE SEX

Cybersex really doesn't mean that much, it's just something that's really fun to do, that leaves no mess, no side effects, and it's the best form of contraception you'll ever find.

 Teen Girl
quoted in Growing Up Digital by Don Tapscott

I have so much cybersex, my baby's first words will be, "You've got mail."

Paulara R. Hawkins
Comedian, Actress

They think they're going to get online and type dirty words and masturbate, but many people find themselves falling in love.... For men and women who don't have that kind of sexual candor in their lives—who never had that freedom to express themselves—when they find someone they can do that with, it's a heavy connection.

Lisa Palac
(1963–) Writer, Editor

It was great, but extremely hard to type with one hand.

25-Year-old Male Respondent
to a *Men's Health* survey; **about online sexual relationships**

The web is a dominatrix. Every where I turn, I see little buttons ordering me to Submit.

Nytwind
Internet User

A WOMAN PEERING AT A MAN SITTING AT HIS LAPTOP COMPUTER: "And just what was that little window you clicked off when I came in?"

 Arnie Levin
Present Day Cartoonist in the *New Yorker*

180

ALTERNATIVE SEX

Insightful Observations on PHONE SEX

To speak of love is to make love.

Honoré de Balzac
(1799–1850) Author

MAN SITTING AT COMPUTER WHILE TALKING ON THE PHONE: "I know it's tech-support, but, for two-fifty a minute, I expect you to talk dirty."

Pat Byrnes
Present Day Cartoonist in the *New Yorker*

What's embarrassing about phone sex is that the neighbors can hear me having sex but they don't see anyone enter or leave the apartment.

Sue Kolinsky
Comedian

I used to make obscene phone calls to her collect—and she used to accept the charges.

Woody Allen
(1935–) Director, Actor, Writer

I was too shy to express my sexual needs except over the phone to someone I don't know.

Garry Shandling
(1949–) Actor, Writer, Comedian

I tried phone sex and it gave me an ear infection.

Richard Lewis
(1947-) Comedian, Actor

All phone calls are obscene.

Karen Elizabeth Gordon
Author, Illustrator

= IDEALIST = REALIST = CYNIC

181

GETTING STARTED

AVOIDING SEX

EXPERIENCING SEX

EXPERIMENTING

COMMON PROBLEMS

SEX AND SOCIETY

ALTERNATIVE SEX

Insightful Observations on
SAME SEX EXPERIMENTING

OK, I've experimented with both sexes but I'm not a limp-wristed floozy and I'm not a transvestite. I'm a very masculine person.

 Boy George
(1961–) Singer; DJ

I have tried sex with both men and women. I found I like it.

Dusty Springfield
(1939–) Singer; Songwriter

There's nothing wrong with going to bed with somebody of your own sex. People should be very free with sex—they should draw the line at goats.

Sir Elton John
(1947–) Rock Singer; Musician

Some women can be completely gay. I'm not one of them. When I do it, though, I like really trashy porno girls. Like porno 44DD, and they have to be really aggressive. Otherwise, why bother?

Courtney Love
(1965–) Singer; Actress

All my sexual experiences when I was young were with girls. I mean we didn't have those sleep-overs for nothing. I think that's really normal; same-sex experimentation.

Madonna
(1958–) Singer; Songwriter; Actress

That was a part of the swinging period of the seventies—I was exploring the outer limits of my sexuality, and it included bisexuality. But I never really had an emotional connection with a man.

 Hugh Hefner
(1926–) Founder of *Playboy*

If you have one gay experience, does that mean you're gay? If you have one heterosexual experience, does that mean you're straight? Life doesn't work quite so cut and dried.

Billie Jean King
(1943–) Tennis Champion

182

Insightful Observations

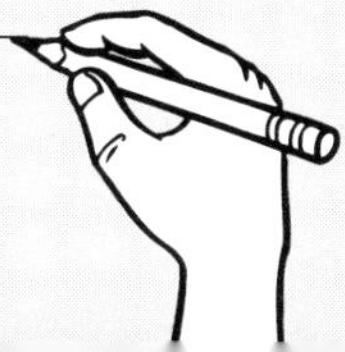

_____

_____

_____

_____

_____

_____

_____

_____

_____

_____

_____

_____

_____

_____

_____

_____

_____

_____

_____

_____

Step Five:

COM
PROB

mon
LEMS

Sex Complaints

Sex Advice

Safe Sex

Cheating

SEX COMPLAINTS

Insightful Observations on
COMPLAINTS FROM WOMEN

All too many men still seem to believe, in a rather naive and egocentric way, that what feels good to them is automatically what feels good to women.

Shere Hite
(1942–) Author

Men are nothing but lazy lumps of drunken flesh. They crowd you in bed, get you all worked up, and then before you can say, Is that all there is? that's all there is.

Latka Gravas's mother
in *Taxi* TV Sitcom (1978–1983)

He always has an orgasm and he doesn't wait for me. He's selfish. I don't think it's fair; so I pulled back the sheets then, and I did it.

Lorena Bobbitt
Housewife; **on why she cut off her husband's penis**

… he twisted my nipples as though tuning a radio.

Lisa Alther
(1944–) Writer

Women complain about sex more often than men. Their gripes fall into two major categories: (1) Not enough. (2) Too much.

Ann Landers
(1918–2002) Advice Columnist

Ouch! You're on my hair!

Sex Manual Title
suggested by Richard Lewis
(1947–) Comedian, Actor

THE GUIDE TO LAUGHING AT SEX

SEX COMPLAINTS

Insightful Observations on
PREMATURE EJACULATION

Premature ejaculation, I don't believe in that. If I come, it was right on time, that's the way I see it. As far as I'm concerned I can't come fast enough. They're mad at me because we have different goals in sex: I'm a speedfucker.

 Author Unknown

It happens to everybody. When it happens to me, I say, "Hey, you know, it's just my way of saying that I'm happy to see you."

 Richard Lewis
(1947–) Comedian, Actor

"Crime of passion"—that phrase drives me crazy. A man murdering his girlfriend is not a crime of passion. Premature ejaculation—that's a crime of passion.

 Dr. Hellura Lyle
Character on the X-Files

 = IDEALIST   = REALIST   = CYNIC

SEX COMPLAINTS

Insightful Observations on
STAMINA

My uncle Murray said, "You're a man if you can make love as long as it takes to cook a chicken."

David Steinberg
(1942–) Comedian, Actor

Just about everything takes longer than it does, except sex.

Jim McGinn
Writer

I'm going to the backseat of my car with the woman I love, and I won't be back for TEN MINUTES.

Homer Simpson
in *The Simpsons* TV series

In no love story I have ever read is a character ever tired. I had to wait for Blanchot for someone to tell me about Fatigue.

Roland Barthes
(1915–1980) Writer, Critic, Teacher

You can improve your endurance by extending foreplay as long as possible, then letting her get on top before making the big rollover. If you play this right, you can drag it out an extra thirty minutes or so.

A Man's Guide to Life
by Stephen Arnott

I like making love myself and I can make love for about three minutes. Three minutes of serious fucking and I need eight hours sleep, and a bowl of Wheaties.

Richard Pryor
(1940–) Comedian, Actor, Writer

One night I made love for an hour and five minutes. It was the day they pushed the clock ahead.

Garry Shandling
(1949–) Actor, Writer, Comedian

188

SEX COMPLAINTS

Insightful Observations on LACK OF SEX

It is not until sex has died out between a man and a woman that they can really love.

😵 **Enid Bagnold**
(1889–1981) Novelist, Playwrite

It's been so long since I made love, I can't remember who gets tied up.

😉 **Joan Rivers**
(1933–) Actress, Comedian

My love life is so bad I am taking part in the world celibacy championships. I meet the Pope in the semi-finals.

🙂 **Guy Bellamy**
Present Day British Novelist

If it weren't for pickpockets, I'd have no sex life at all.

😊 **Rodney Dangerfield**
(1921–) Actor, Comedian

The only reason I would take up jogging is so that I could hear heavy breathing again.

😊 **Erma Bombeck**
(1927–1996) Humorist, Author

These days I am sleeping alone. Sometimes I wake up in the middle of the night, put on my blue eye shadow and try to learn country dancing in front of the TV.

😊 **Cybill Shepherd**
(1950–) Actress

The last time I was inside a woman was when I visited the Statue of Liberty.

😊 **Woody Allen**
(1935–) Director, Actor, Writer

SEX COMPLAINTS

Insightful Observations on
REGRETS

MICHELLE PFEIFFER: Why didn't we do this before?
ROBERT REDFORD: Because it was always going to be this hard to stop.

Up Close and Personal
(1996) written by John Gregory Dunne & Joan Didion

I was very hungry in my younger days. Starving. Out of my mind.... I'd just like to think, "What a waste of time, not being a slut!"

Kim Basinger
(1953–) Actress

I had sex with a woman I shouldn't have, OK? And she was a prostitute.

Jerry Springer
(1944–) Talk Show Host

Sex with an ex can be depressing. If it's good, you don't have it anymore. If it's bad, you just had sex with an ex.

Kim Cattrall
in HBO's *Sex and the City*

Sex changes things. I've had relationships where I know a guy and then I have sex with him and then I bump into him someplace and he acts like I loaned him money.

Teri Garr
in *Tootsie* (1982)

As she lay there dozing next to me, one voice inside my head kept saying, "Relax ... you are not the first doctor to sleep with one of his patients," but another kept reminding me, "Howard, you are a veterinarian."

Dick Wilson
(1916–) Actor

190

SEX COMPLAINTS

Insightful Observations on
IMPOTENCE

Someone asked Sophocles, How do you feel now about sex? Are you still able to have a woman? He replied, Hush, man; most glad indeed I am to be rid of it all, as though I had escaped from a mad and savage master.

Sophocles
(496–406 B.C.) Greek Dramatist

CHARLOTTE: We're having Trey's sperm tested.
MIRANDA: Is it not doing well in school?

Kristin Davis and Cynthia Nixon
in HBO's Sex and the City

The latest news on this new impotency drug Viagra. Some insurance companies won't pay unless men can prove that they're impotent. Which means that men are at a disadvantage if they have a really hot pharmacist.

Conan O'Brien
(1963–) Humorist, Talk Show Host

I'm going to Iowa for an award, Carnegie Hall to France to be honored—I'd give it all up for one erection.

Groucho Marx
(1890–1977) Humorist, Actor

Though a man may be a dignified judge, a captain of industry, a national golf champion, or a distinguished physicist, he feels worthless and debased if he cannot perform an act which he shares in common with dogs, rabbits, cattle, and rats.

Howard R. and Martha E. Lewis
Authors, Sex Health Experts

What a jolly bunch they were, and the only one who wasn't smiling was Solly, a 70-year-old taxi driver, who was staring mournfully at his prick and intoning: We were born together. We grew up together. We got married together. Why, oh why, did you have to die before me?

Jeffrey Bernard
(1932–1997) English Writer

INSIGHTFUL OBSERVATIONS TO SHARE

SEX COMPLAINTS

Insightful Observations on
SEX & HONESTY

Whatever deceives seems to produce magical enchantment.

Plato
(427–348 B.C.) Greek Philosopher

I never said I love you. I don't care about I love you. I read the Second Sex. I read The Cinderella Complex. I'm responsible for my own orgasm. I don't care. I just don't want to be lied to.

Teri Garr
in *Tootsie* (1982)

I would say that the sexual organs express the human soul more than any other limb of the body. They are not diplomats. They tell the truth ruthlessly.

Isaac Bashevis
(1904–1991) Singer, Writer

There is nothing like desire for preventing the thing one says from bearing any resemblance to what one has in mind.

Phyllis Diller
(1917–) Comedian, Actress, Author

Honesty had ruined more marriages than infidelity.

Jimmy Williams
Writer, Actor, Producer

Everyone lies about sex, more or less, to themselves if not to others, to others if not to themselves, exaggerating its importance or minimizing its pull.

Daphne Merkin
Writer, Editor, Sex Columnist

The only people who make love all the time are liars.

Telly Savalas
(1922–1994) Actor

192

SEX COMPLAINTS

Insightful Observations on
HONEST MEN

If I'm not interested in a woman, I'm straight-forward. Right after sex, I usually say, "I can't do this anymore. Thanks for coming over."

😎 **Vince Vaughn**
(1970–) Actor, Writer

There is nothing about which men lie so much as their sexual powers. In this at least every man is, what in his heart he would like to be, a Casanova.

😊 **W. Somerset Maugham**
(1874–1965) Writer

If a man tells a woman she's beautiful, she'll overlook most of his other lies.

😊 **Author Unknown**

WOMAN TALKING TO A MAN IN BED AFTER SEX: "Be honest, are you seeing someone else, or did you get that from 'Men's Health'?"

😊 **Marisa Acocella**
Present Day Cartoonist in the *New Yorker*

Men who betray woman also betray other men. Women shouldn't feel so special.

😊 **Garry Shandling**
(1949–) Actor, Writer, Comedian

Woe to the man who tries to be frank in lovemaking.

😊 **George Sand**
(1804–1876) French Novelist, Early Feminist

SEX COMPLAINTS

Insightful Observations on
HONEST WOMEN

There is no sincerity like a woman telling a lie.

 Cecil Parker
about Ingrid Bergman in
Indiscreet (1958) written by
Norman Krasna

I feel so guilty—he's my husband—he trusts me. If he didn't trust me I couldn't do this.

 Elaine May
(1932-) Writer, Actress;
*Sketch about an Adulterous
Wife*

Honest women are inconsolable for the mistakes they haven't made.

 Sacha Guitry
(1885-1957) French
Playwrite, Actor

Ever since Adam, men have rolled over onto their side of the bed, lit a cigarette, and asked, "what were you thinking about?" And the woman has answered, "Nothing." Or the more outspoken, "You." How can men have really believed them all this time?

 Nancy Friday
(1937-) Writer, Pychologist

THE GUIDE TO LAUGHING AT SEX

SEX COMPLAINTS

Insightful Observations on
MARRIAGE & SEX

They say the best exercise takes place in the bedroom. I believe it, because that's where I get the most resistance.

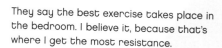 **Jeff Shaw**
(1966–) Comedian

Some nights he said he was tired, and some nights she said she wanted to read, and other nights no one said anything.

Joan Didion
(1934–) Writer

More divorces start in the bedroom than in any other room in the house.

Ann Landers
(1918–2002) Advice Columnist

You know how the military will bomb the enemy to weaken their defenses before they invade? I send love letters to my wife for the same reason.

Oscar Herman
(1909–1980) Humorist, Shoe Salesman

The total amount of undesired sex endured by women is probably greater in marriage than in prostitution.

Bertrand Rusell
(1872–1970) Mathematician, Philosopher

Both of my ex-wives closed their eyes when making love because they didn't want to see me having a good time.

Joseph Wambaugh
(1937–) Author

Marriage is like a bank account. You put it in, you take it out, you lose interest.

Professor Irwin Corey
(1912–) Comedian

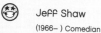 = IDEALIST   = REALIST   😃 = CYNIC

195

GETTING STARTED

AVOIDING SEX

EXPERIENCING SEX

EXPERIMENTING

COMMON PROBLEMS

SEX AND SOCIETY

SEX COMPLAINTS

Insightful Observations on
AGING & SEX

I'm sixty-nine-years-old, I have two children: one's four and one's three, and it was done without Viagra.

Larry King
(1933–) Writer, Talk Show Host

I can't wait to get Alzheimer's—new pussy every night!

Bobby Slayton
(1951-) Comedian

Oh, to be seventy again!

Oliver Wendell Holmes
(1841–1935) Attorney; **said in his eighty-seventh year while watching a pretty girl.**

A man is only as old as the woman he feels.

Groucho Marx
(1890–1977) Humorist, Actor

Sex after ninety is like trying to shot pool with a rope. Even putting my cigar in its holder is a thrill.

George Burns
(1896–1996) Comedian, Actor

THE GUIDE TO LAUGHING AT SEX

SEX COMPLAINTS

Insightful Observations on
AGING & DESIRE

You'll have to ask somebody older than me.

Eubie Blake
(1883–1983) Composer; **age
ninety, when asked at what
age the sex drive ends**

As long as a person does not give up sex, sex does not give up a person.

Gabriel Garcia
Marquez
(1928–) Author

Sex can be fun after eighty, after ninety, and after lunch.

George Burns
(1896–1996) Comedian,
Actor

Sad to admit my age is showing.
I fear my days of coming are going.

Gardner E. Lewis
Humorist

GETTING STARTED

AVOIDING SEX

EXPERIENCING SEX

EXPERIMENTING

COMMON PROBLEMS

SEX AND SOCIETY

SEX COMPLAINTS

Insightful Observations on
SEXUAL DIFFERENCES
MEN & WOMEN

Women need a reason to have sex, men just need a place.

Billy Crystal
(1947–) Actor, Comedian

Women are the most powerful magnet in the universe. And all men are cheap metal. And we all know where North is.

Larry Miller
(1953–) Comedian, Actor

Seems to me the basic conflict between men and women, sexually, is that men are like firemen. To men, sex is an emergency, and no matter what we're doing we can be ready in two minutes. Women, on the other hand, are like fire. They're very exciting, but the conditions have to be exactly right for it to occur.

Jerry Seinfeld
(1954–) Comedian, Actor

In general, I think it's true that women fuck to love and men love to fuck.

Carrie Fisher
(1956–) Actress, Writer

Man makes love by braggadocio, and woman makes love by listening.

H.L. Mencken
(1880–1956) Editor, Writer

There is more difference within the sexes than between them.

Dame Ivy Compton-Burnett
(1884–1969) Writer

198

SEX ADVICE

Insightful Observations on
SEX ADVICE

Some tickling or telling funny stories in bed can make sex more interesting.

Dr. Ruth Westheimer
(1928–) Psychologist, Author, Sex Counselor

When things don't work well in the bedroom, they don't work well in the living room either.

Dr. William H. Masters
(1915–2001) Biologist, Sexual Therapist; Masters & Johnson Institute

The thing that takes up the least amount of time and causes the most amount of trouble …

John Barrymore
(1882–1942) Actor

After being alive, the next hardest work is sex. Some people get energy from sex, and some people lose energy from sex. I have found that it's too much work. But if you have the time for it, and if you need the exercise—then you should do it.

Andy Warhol
(1928–1987) Pop Artist, Film Maker

If sex is such a natural phenomenon, how come there are so many books on how to do it?

Bette Midler
(1944–) Actress, Singer, Comedian

MARRIAGE COUNSELOR SPEAKS TO A COUPLE:
"Maybe you ought to consider making love in the morning—before you have a chance to piss each other off."

Robert Mankoff
Present Day Cartoonist in the *New Yorker*

No problem is so big or so complicated that it can't be run away from.

Charles Schulz
(1922–2000) Cartoonist; "Peanuts"

INSIGHTFUL OBSERVATIONS TO SHARE

199

SEX ADVICE

Insightful Observations on
SEX ADVICE
FOR MEN

Check the oil and ring the bell.

John Leguizamo
(1964–) Actor, Writer;
advice from his aunt and
gay uncle on sex

A nuclear reactor is just like a woman, all
you have to do is read the manual and push
the right buttons.

Homer Simpson
in *The Simpsons* TV Show

There is very little advice in men's magazines
because men think, I know what I'm doing.
Just show me somebody naked.

Jerry Seinfeld
(1954–) Comedian, Actor

My advice is to look to the big picture: by
expressing devotion to one woman you are
setting yourself up in very good graces with
the queen bee. And her rewards are
historically proven to be far more sensuous
than a quick lay.

Thurston Moore
(1958–) Musician

Stay away from girls who cry or who look
like they get pregnant easily.

P.J. O'Rourke
(1947–) Humorist,
Journalist

Have you heard of this new book entitled
1,001 Sex Secrets Men Should Know? It
contains comments from 1,001 women on how
men can be better in bed. I think that women
would actually settle for three: slow down,
turn off the TV, call out the right name.

Jay Leno
(1950–) Comedian, Talk
Show Host

200

SEX ADVICE

Insightful Observations on SEX ADVICE FOR WOMEN

WOMAN TO MAN, REFERRING TO MAGAZINE SHE IS READING: "There's an article in here that explains why you're such an idiot."

William Haefeli
Present Day Cartoonist in the *New Yorker*

MIRANDA: I don't know ... is it okay to fuck one guy when you're pregnant with another guy's baby?
CARRIE: If one more person asks me that today ...

Cynthia Nixon & Sarah Jessica Parker
in HBO's *Sex and the City*

Don't confide in your girlfriends.... If you let them advise you, they'll see to it in the name of friendship that you lose your husband and your home. I'm an old woman, my dear. I know my sex.

Lucile Watson
in *The Women* (1939) written by Anita Loos & Jane Murfin, novel by Clare Boothe Luce

Self-help books are making life downright unsafe. Women desperate to catch a man practice all the ploys recommended by these authors. Bump into him, trip over him, knock him down, spill something on him, scald him, but meet him.

Florence King
(1936–) Author

If a man comes to your front door saying he is conducting a survey and asks you to show him your boobs, do not show him your boobs! This is a scam, and he is only trying to see your boobs.

Newsweek
on e-mail warnings

SEX ADVICE

Insightful Observations on SEX THERAPY

My method is basically the same as Masters and Johnson, only they charge thousands of dollars and it's called therapy. I charge fifty dollars and it's called prostitution.

Xaviera Hollander
(1943–) Madam, Writer

There a two things no man will admit he can't do well—drive and make love.

Stirling Moss
(1929–) Race Car Driver

Look, I can't promise I'll change, but I can promise I'll pretend to change.

Robert Mankoff
Present Day Cartoonist in the *New Yorker*

Dr. Ruth says that, as women, we should tell our lovers how to make love to us. My boyfriend goes nuts if I tell him how to drive.

Pam Stone
Comedian, Actress

There's nothing wrong with a person's sex life that the psychoanalyst can't exaggerate.

Gerald Horton Bath
Writer

I have a tremendous fear of intimacy. I feel luck just to get aroused, because my penis is usually in the shape of a question mark. If I'm lucky enough to get an erection, fortunately for me, my hard-on points to the nearest counseling center.

Richard Lewis
(1947–) Comedian, Actor

202

SEX ADVICE

Insightful Observations on
SEXUAL COMPATIBILITY

We haven't worked out all our problems, but the sex is better than ever.

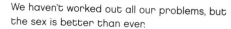

Pamela Anderson Lee
(1967–) Actress; **on reuniting with her then husband, Tommy Lee**

PSYCHIATRIST: How often do you sleep together?
WOODY ALLEN: Hardly ever, maybe three times a week.
DIANE KEATON: Constantly, I'd say three times a week.

Woody Allen and Diane Keaton
Annie Hall (1977) written by Woody Allen & Marshall Brickman

It was an old quandary for them. He needed sex in order to feel connected to her, and she needed to feel connected to him in order to enjoy sex.

Lisa Alther
(1944–) Writer

A young man who grows up expecting to dominate sexually is bound to be somewhat startled by a young woman who wants sex as much as he does, and multi-orgasmic sex at that.

Nora Ephron
(1941–) Writer, Director

If it happens that you like peanut butter in bed while you're having sex and your partner doesn't, in the long run the thing to do may be to find another partner.

Dr. Ruth Westheimer
(1928–) Psychologist, Author; Sex Counselor

Men reach their sexual peak at eighteen. Women reach their sexual peak at thirty-five. Do you get the feeling God is into practical jokes? We're reaching our sexual peak right around the same time they're discovering they have a favorite chair.

Rita Rudner
(1956–) Comedian

😆 = IDEALIST   😊 = REALIST   🙂 = CYNIC

203

SEX ADVICE

Insightful Observations on

TALKING ABOUT SEX

Did you know that we ladies have bull sessions ... among ourselves, and we talk about which of you fellas are good stud service and which of you aren't? If you boys knew what you sound like when you and your bedroom manners are dissected ... it would curl your hair, because we talk about exactly the same things you do among yourselves—and just as graphically.

Madalyn Murray
(1923–) World's best-known Atheist

All really great lovers are articulate, and verbal seduction is the surest road to actual seduction.

Marya Mannes
(1904–1990) Journalist

We women as naturally love a scandal as you men do debauchery; and we can no more keep up conversation without one, than you can live an age without t'other.

Mary Davys
(1674–1732) Poet, Novelist, Playwrite

Sex has become one of the most discussed subjects of modern times. The Victorians pretended it did not exist; the moderns pretend that nothing else exists.

Bishop Fulton J. Sheen
(1895–1979) Catholic Prelate

Sex is like money—very nice to have but vulgar to talk about.

Tonia Berg
Humorist

There's nothing left to talk about, unless it's horizontally. • Let's get physical, physical. I wanna get physical. Let's get into physical. • Let me hear your body talk, your body talk. Let me hear your body talk.

Olivia Newton-John
"Physical," words and music by Stephen Kipner & Terry Shaddick

204

SEX ADVICE

Insightful Observations on
SEX & COMPROMISE

When the Prince of Wales, later to be King Edward VII, said to his mistress, Lily Langtry, during a quarrel, that "I've spent enough on you to buy a battleship," she replied, "And you've spent enough in me to float one."

 Author Unknown

Men need sexual fulfillment in order to respond to a woman emotionally; woman need emotional fulfillment to respond to a man sexually.

Ellen Krieg
Writer

In real life, women are always trying to mix something up with sex—religion, babies, or hard cash; it is only men who long for sex separated out, without rings or strings.

Katherine Whitehorn
(1928–) Columnist, Author

Marriage is the price men pay for sex; sex is the price women pay for marriage.

Author Unknown

Men have been trained and conditioned by women, not unlike the way Pavlov conditioned his dogs, into becoming their slaves. As compensation for their labors, men are given periodic use of women's vaginas.

Esther Vilar
(1935–) Playwrite

A woman sometimes fucks without discrimination just to get out of a situation. She thinks, "Oh my god, I really don't want to fuck this man, but if I sit here and argue for the next six hours trying to talk this turd out of it, I'll be a rag tomorrow." So she says, "I want to go to bed, I'm tired. But if you're fucking going to insist, if you're going to keep me here all night, then I'll lie on the floor with my legs apart and think of something else and you can fuck me, you stupid swine. Then I'll be able to go to sleep"

Germaine Greer
(1939–) Feminist, Writer, Lecturer

WELLNESS THROUGH LAUGHTER

SAFE SEX

Insightful Observations on
PROTECTION

Contraceptives should be used on every conceivable occasion.

 Spike Milligan
(1918–2002) British Comic, Actor, Author

It's still fun to be single. You just have to be more careful. Your date comes to the door, you say, I'm sewing this button on my jacket—oops, pricked your finger—I'll get a slide.

 Elayne Boosler
(1952–) Comedian

I'm scared of sex now. You have to be. You can get something terminal, like a kid.

 Wendy Liebman
(1961–) Comedian

The best contraceptive for old people is nudity.

 Phyllis Diller
(1917–) Comedian, Actress, Author

When I was giving birth, the nurse asked, Still think blonds have more fun?

 Joan Rivers
(1933–) Actress, Comedian

THE GUIDE TO LAUGHING AT SEX

SAFE SEX

Insightful Observations on
SAFE SEX

Remember when Safe Sex meant your parents had gone away for the weekend?

 Rhonda Hansome
Actress, Writer

Who would have ever thought you could die from sex? It was much more fun when you only went to hell.

John Waters
(1946–) Actor, Writer

For the first time in history, sex is more dangerous than the cigarette afterwards.

Jay Leno
(1950–) Comedian, Talk Show Host

Safe sex is very important. That's why I'm never doing it on a plywood scaffolding again.

Jenny Jones
(1946–) Talk Show Host

Despite a lifetime of service to the cause of sexual liberation I have never caught a venereal disease, which makes me feel rather like an arctic explorer who has never had frostbite.

Germaine Greer
(1939–) Feminist, Writer, Lecturer

Wouldn't it be great if we found you could only get AIDS from giving money to TV preachers?

Elayne Boosler
(1952–) Comedian

SAFE SEX

Insightful Observations on
ORAL CONTRACEPTION

The Pill came to market and changed the sexual and real-estate habits of millions; motel chains were created to serve them.

 Herbert Gold
Comedian

I want to tell you a terrific story about oral contraception. I asked this girl to sleep with me and she said no.

 Woody Allen
(1935–) Director, Actor, Writer

For a single woman, the most effective method of oral contraception is to just yell out, Yes, yes, I want to have your baby!!!

 Marsha Doble
Comedian

That's why I still take the Pill. I don't want any more grandchildren.

 Phyllis Diller
(1917–) Comedian, Actress, Author

208

SAFE SEX

Insightful Observations on CONDOMS

Condoms should be marketed in three sizes, jumbo, colossal, and super colossal, so that men do not have to go in and ask for the small.

 Barbara Seaman
Author

National Condom Week is coming soon. Hey, there's a parade you don't want to miss.

Jay Leno
(1950–) Comedian, Talk Show Host

There's a new medical crisis. Doctors are reporting that many men are having allergic reactions to latex condoms. They say they cause severe swelling. So what's the problem?

Dustin Hoffman
(1937–) Actor

Always have condoms around. It's not presumptuous, it's necessary. It's like your quart of milk. People always buy milk, even if they don't like it, because who doesn't buy milk? Same with condoms.

Rachael Klein
University of California, Berkeley Sex Columnist

You never really know a guy until you ask him to wear a rubber.

Madonna
(1958–) Singer, Songwriter, Actress

Condoms aren't completely safe. A friend of mine was wearing one and got hit by a bus.

 Bob Rubin
Comedian

SAFE SEX

Insightful Observations on
RELIGION & BIRTH CONTROL

It is now quite lawful for a Catholic woman to avoid pregnancy by resorting to mathematics, though she is still forbidden to resort to physics or chemistry.

H.L. Mencken
(1880–1956) Editor, Writer;
on the rhythm method

The command 'Be fruitful and multiply' was promulgated according to our authorities when the population of the world consisted of two people.

Dean Inge
(1860–1954) British
Churchman.

Protestant women may take the Pill. Roman Catholic women must keep taking the Tablet.

Irene Thomas
(1920–) British Writer

He no play-a da game. He no make-a da rules!

Earl Butz
(1909–) U.S. Politician;
referring to the Pope's
strictures against
contraception

CHEATING

Insightful Observations on
CODES OF FIDELITY

CARRIE: Well, I think maybe there's a cheating curve. That someone's definition of what constitutes cheating is in direct proportion to how much they themselves want to cheat.

MIRANDA: That's moral relativism!

CARRIE: I prefer to think of it as quantum cheating.

HBO's *Sex and the City*

Sammy Davis Jr. had his own code of marital fidelity. He explained to me that he could do anything with me except have normal intercourse because that would be cheating on his wife.

Linda Lovelace
(1949–2002) Porn Star

He sued for divorce on the most serious grounds of all—adultery. I didn't think that was fair. Tammy wasn't wearing his ring the first time she and I made love. I had taken it off her personally.

George Jones
(1931–) Country Singer; on **Tammy Wynette's husband**

Monogamy is the Western custom of one wife and hardly any mistresses.

Saki
(1870–1916) Writer

A man can have two or maybe three love affairs while he is married. After that it is cheating.

Yves Montand
(1921–1991) French Actor, Singer

We've been married for eleven years and not once have I been unfaithful to her in the same city.

George Segal
in *A Touch of Class* (1973) written by Melvin Frank & Jack Rose

😇 = IDEALIST   😊 = REALIST   😏 = CYNIC

211

CHEATING

Insightful Observations on
CHEATING

The world wants to be cheated. So cheat.

 Xaviera Hollander
(1943–) Madam, Writer

If our elaborate and dominating bodies are given us to be denied at every turn, if our nature is always wrong and wicked, how ineffectual we are—like fishes not meant to swim.

 Cyril Connolly
(1903–1974) British Journalist

Marriage without infidelity is like salad without dressing.

 Keith Waterhouse
(1929–) British Playwrite

Even a rat likes to go into a different hole once in a while.

 Author Unknown

Monogamy is monogamy until you screw someone else.

 River Phoenix
(1970–1993) Actor

A man with one watch knows what time it is. A man with two watches is never sure.

 John Peers
Humorist

For a whore is a deep ditch; and a strange woman is a narrow pit.

 The Holy Bible

212

CHEATING

Insightful Observations on EXTRAMARITAL AFFAIRS

Do infants enjoy infancy as much as adults enjoy adultery?

😵 **George Carlin**
(1938–) Comedian, Actor, Writer

So heavy is the chain of wedlock that it needs two to carry it, and sometimes three.

😵 **Alexandre Dumas**
(1802–1870) French Writer

Adultery can be a more healthy recreation than, for example, the game of mah-jongg or watching television.

😵 **Dr. Albert Ellis**
(1869–1951) Businessman

In Europe, extramarital affairs are considered a sign of good health, a feat.

😵 **Jean-Pierre Detremmerie**
on Bill Clinton's alleged affairs

You know, of course, that the Tasmanians, who never committed adultery, are now extinct.

😵 **W. Somerset Maugham**
(1874–1965) Writer

A study of 853 human societies turned up this: the practice where each man has only one wife is normal in only 16%.

😃 **Elizabeth Joseph**
(1828–1906) Social Reformer

Adultery may or may not be sinful, but it is never cheap.

😃 **Raymond Postgate**
(1896–1971) Writer, Historian

CHEATING

Insightful Observations on
OPEN RELATIONSHIPS

I've never bought that open marriage thing. I've never seen it work. But that doesn't mean I believe in monogamy. Sleeping with someone else doesn't necessarily constitute infidelity.

 Carly Simon
(1945–) Singer, Songwriter

I haven't known any open marriages although quite a few have been ajar.

 Zsa Zsa Gabor
(1917–) Hungarian Actress

MATT DILLON: Look, Janet, you know I see other people still. You do know that don't you?
BRIDGITTE FONDA: You don't fool me.
MATT DILLON: Janet, I could not be fooling you less.

 Singles
(1992) Written by Cameron Crowe

Penguins mate for life. Which doesn't exactly surprise me that much 'cause they all look alike—it's not like they're gonna meet a better-looking penguin someday.

 Ellen Degeneres
(1958–) Comedian

An open marriage is nature's way of telling you that you need a divorce.

 Ann Landers
(1918–2002) Advice Columnist

THE GUIDE TO LAUGHING AT SEX

CHEATING

Insightful Observations on
MEN CHEATING

Should a man in private be without control or guidance in his pleasures and commit some indiscretion with a prostitute or servant girl, the wife should consider this a sign of his respect for her; that he does not include her in his drunken parties, excesses and wantonness with other women.

   Plutarch
(47–120 AD) Historian, Philosopher

A man is only as faithful as his options.

   Chris Rock
(1966–) Humorist, Comedian, Actor

What I don't, like, get is how she, like, figured out I was, like, having an affair with, like, the babysitter.

   Danny Shanahan
Present Day Cartoonist in the *New Yorker*

We women are so much more sensible. When we tire of ourselves, we change the way we do our hair, or hire a new cook, or decorate the house. I suppose a man could do over his office, but he never thinks of anything so simple. No, dear, a man has only one escape from his old self—to see a different self in the mirror of some woman's eyes.

   Lucile Watson
in *The Women* (1939) written by Anita Loos and Jane Murfin, novel by Clare Boothe Luce

He had lied to me. The bastard was cheating on me—with his wife!

   Joan Collins
(1933–) Actress; on **producer George England**

Eighty percent of married men cheat in America. The rest cheat in Europe.

   Jackie Mason
(1934–) Comedian

CHEATING

Insightful Observations on WOMEN CHEATING

Suddenly and ironically, she was becoming the kind of woman he had long idealized in his fantasies—the daring, carefree, sexually liberated woman he had searched for.

 Gay Talese
(1932–) Writer; **on a man discovering his wife's infidelity:**

Affairs are all right. Just be insanely careful not to have your husband find out.

 Helen Gurly Brown
(1922–) Author, Editor

The woman who is adulterous in her own home must always remember one thing—put the seat down.

 William Cole
(1919–2000) Author

It's very disappointing and hurtful. How come nobody ever thought I had an affair with anyone?

 Barbara Bush
(1925–) Former First Lady; **on Washington scandals**

Bigamy is having one husband too many. Monogamy is the same.

 Erica Jong
(1942–) Writer, Poet

CHEATING

Insightful Observations on OTHER LOVERS

DICK FORAN: Aren't you forgetting that you're married?
MAE WEST: I'm doing my best.

My Little Chickadee
(1940) written by W.C. Fields & Mae West

The difference between my wife and my mistress is the difference between night and day.

Harry Hirshfield
Comedian

To have a new mistress is a pleasure only surpassed by that of ridding yourself of an old one.

William Wycherley
(1640–1716) Playwright

A woman we love rarely satisfies all our needs, and we deceive her with a woman whom we do not love.

Marcel Proust
(1871–1922) French Novelist

BARBARA STANWYCK: Last time I looked, you had a wife.
ROBERT RYAN: Maybe next time you look, I won't.
BS: That's what they all say.

Clash by Night
(1952) written by Alfred Hayes, play by Clifford Odets

GETTING STARTED

AVOIDING SEX

EXPERIENCING SEX

EXPERIMENTING

COMMON PROBLEMS

SEX AND SOCIETY

CHEATING

Insightful Observations on
GETTING AWAY WITH CHEATING

Love means never having to say you're sorry.

 Ali MacGraw
to Ryan O'Neal in *Love Story* (1970) written by Erich Segal

Adultery: Second only to front-line combat, produces feats of almost lunatic daring. And it thrives on the extraordinary capacity of the deceived partner to ignore the signs of infidelity so obvious to the rest of the world.

 Mary Beard
(1876–1958) Historian, Social Reformer

The first man that can think up a good explanation how he can be in love with his wife and another woman is going to win that prize they're always giving out in Sweden.

 Mary Cecil
in *The Women* (1939)

Never tell. Not if you love your wife.... In fact, if your old lady walks in on you, deny it. Yeah. Just flat out and she'll believe it: I'm tellin' ya. This chick came downstairs with a sign around her neck, 'Lay On Top Of Me Or I'll Die.' I didn't know what I was gonna do ...

 Lenny Bruce
(1925–1966) Comedian

218

Insightful Observations

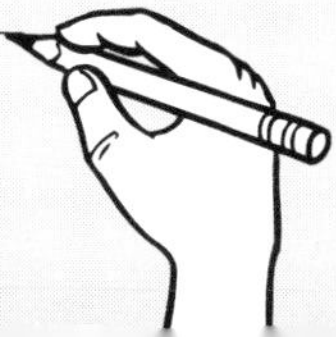

_____

_____

_____

_____

_____

_____

_____

_____

_____

_____

_____

_____

_____

_____

_____

_____

😖 = IDEALIST   😔 = REALIST   🙂 = CYNIC

Step Six:

SEX

SOC

AND
IETY

OUR CULTURE

Insightful Observations on
SEX & SOCIETY

Sexuality is the great battle between biology and society.

😋 **Nancy Friday**
(1937–) Writer, Psychologist

Our society treats sex as a sport, with its record breakers, its judges, its rules and its spectators.

😋 **Susan Lydon**
Present Day Author; *The Politics of Orgasm*

Sex gets people killed, put in jail, beaten up, bankrupted, and disgraced, to say nothing of ruined—personally, politically, and professionally. Looking for sex can lead to misfortune, and if you get lucky and find it, it can leave you maimed, infected, or dead. Other than that, it's swell; the great American pastime.

😃 **Edna Buchanan**
(1939–) Crime Reporter, Mystery Writer

The orgasm has replaced the Cross as the focus of longing and the image of fulfillment.

😊 **Malcolm Muggeridge**
(1903–1990) Journalist, Sage

If all the young ladies who attended the Yale promenade dance were laid end to end, no one would be the least surprised.

🙂 **Dorothy Parker**
(1893–1967) Writer

THE GUIDE TO LAUGHING AT SEX

OUR CULTURE

Insightful Observations on
BEING BISEXUAL

If you swing both ways, you really swing … double your pleasure.

 Joan Baez
(1941–) Folk Singer, Songwriter

I date men and women. What Woody Allen said was true. Say what you will about bisexuality, you have a fifty percent better chance of finding a date on Saturday night.

 David Geffen
(1943–) Film, Music Executive

Ever since I had that interview in which I said I was bisexual, it seems twice as many people wave at me in the streets.

Sir Elton John
(1947–) Rock Singer, Musician

Because our society is so polarized between heterosexuals and homosexuals, the bisexual closet has two doors.

Loraine Hutchins and Lani Kaahuanu
Authors

Bisexuality is not so much a cop-out as a fearful compromise.

Jill Johnston
Writer

Bisexuals … are incredibly greedy MF's…. Get off the fence and pick a hole.

Dennis Miller
(1953–) Actor, Comedian

 = IDEALIST   = REALIST   = CYNIC

OUR CULTURE

Insightful Observations on
BEING GAY

Tchaikovsky thought of committing suicide for fear of being discovered as a homosexual; but today, if you are a composer and not a homosexual, you might as well put a bullet through your head.

 Diaghilev
(1872–1929) Ballet Impressario

The Bible contains 6 admonishments to homosexuals and 362 admonishments to heterosexuals. That doesn't mean that God doesn't love heterosexuals. It's just that they need more supervision.

 Lynn Lavner
Comedian

The love that previously dared not speak its name has now grown hoarse from screaming.

 Robert Brustein
(1927–) Critic, Theater Director

I'd rather be black than gay because when you're black you don't have to tell your mother.

 Charles Pierce
(1926–1999) Actor, Nightclub Performer

It has been proven that the pig is the only homosexual animal. As this perversion is most prevalent in pork-eating nations, it is obvious that it gets into your genes through the meat.

 Tasleem Ahmed
Islamic Missionary

The worst part of being gay in the twentieth century is all that damn disco music to which one has to listen.

 Quentin Crisp
(1908–1999) Writer

A man talking on phone: "We're not doing anything for Gay Pride this year. We're here, we're queer, we're used to it."

 William Haefeli
Present Day Cartoonist in the *New Yorker*

224

OUR CULTURE

Insightful Observations on
GAY MEN

Most of my male friends are gay and that seems perfectly natural to me. I mean, who wouldn't like penis?

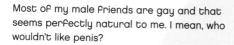 **Valerie Perrine**
(1943–) Actress, Showgirl

I want more in life than meeting a pretty face and sitting down on it.

Harvey Fierstein
(1954–) Playwright, Actor

Rub-a-dub-dub
Three men in a tub
And that's on a slow night.

Posted Sign
in a San Francisco bath
house

Tell a thousand jokes and no one will call you a comedian; suck one dick and your gay.

Neil Gold
(1962–) Humorist; Advice to his younger brother

Almost all the people sunning themselves on the sand were male and usually scantily clad, in that their trunks were the kind I used to call handkerchiefs full of apples. Seen from behind, their buttocks mooned quite bare and strangely pale.

Germaine Greer
(1939) Feminist, Writer; Lecturer

It doesn't matter what the dear boys do so long as they don't do it in the street and frighten the horses.

Mrs. Patrick Campbell
(1865–1940) British Actress

I was asked if my first sexual experience was homosexual or heterosexual. I said I was too polite to ask.

Gore Vidal
(1925–) Novelist, Playwright, Essayist

OUR CULTURE

Insightful Observations on
GAY WOMEN

Want to know why girls turn from straight to gay? Because the sex is great.

Anne Heche
(1969–) Actress, Writer

Once you know what women are like, men get kind of boring. I'm not trying to put them down, I mean I like them sometimes as people, but sexually they're dull.

Rita Mae Brown
(1944–) Writer

Have I lived an alternate lifestyle? The answer is no.

Donna Shalala
(1941–) Political Scientist, Cabinet Officer; **on whether or not she is gay**

I resent like hell that I was maybe eighteen before I ever heard the "L" word. It would have made all the difference for me had I grown up knowing that the reason I didn't fit in was because they hadn't told me there were more categories to fit into.

Michelle Shocked
(1962–) Singer, Songwriter

I think God is a callous bitch not making me a lesbian. I'm deeply disappointed by my sexual interest in men.

Diamanda Galas
(1955–) Singer, Songwriter

I don't think she's a lesbian, I think she just ran out of men.

Kristin Davis
in HBO's *Sex and the City*

226

OUR CULTURE

Insightful Observations on
MUSIC & SEX

My inspiration is right below my waist and in between my legs.

Jon Bon Jovi
(1962–) Singer, Songwriter

Rock is really about dick and testosterone. I go see a band. I want to fuck the guy. That's the way it is. It's always been that way.

Courtney Love
(1965–) Singer, Actress

I would like to play for audiences who are not using my music to stimulate their sex organs.

Ornette Coleman
(1930–) Saxophonist

All my songs are about sex. Nashville likes to pretend it doesn't exist. They should loosen up. Everyone's doing it, aren't they?

Mindy McCready
(1975–) Singer, Songwriter

A lot of tunes in the guise of romanticism have mainly fucking behind them.

Randy Newman
(1943–) Singer, Songwriter, Composer

Classic Van Halen made you want to drink, dance, and fuck. Current Van Halen encourages us to drink milk, drive a Nissan, and have a relationship.

David Lee Roth
(1955–) Singer, Songwriter

OUR CULTURE

Insightful Observations on
SEX SCANDALS

Anyone who knows Dan Quayle knows he would rather play golf than have sex any day.

Marilyn Quayle
Wife of Dan Quayle;
**defending alligations that
Dan had an affair.**

I rowed us to a secluded spot. Right there, the estranged First Lady of Canada lent new meaning to the term head of state.

Geraldo Rivera
(1943–) Television
Journalist; **on his alleged
affair with Margaret
Trudeau**

Madame, you must really be more careful. Suppose it had been someone else who found you like this.

Duc de Richelieu
(1766–1822) French
Statesman; **discovering his
wife with her lover**

That's garbage. Why can't they catch me in a sex scandal. I could use some good publicity.

Willie Brown
(1934–) Speaker, California
Assembly; **responding to
allegations of graft.**

Men in power always seem to get involved in sex scandals but women don't even have a word for "male bimbo." Except maybe "senator."

Elayne Boosler
(1952–) Comedian

OUR CULTURE

Insightful Observations on
POLITICIANS & SEX

May you be as rich as a Republican and have the sex life of a Democrat.

 Johnny Carson
(1925–) Comedian, Talk Show Host

DOCTOR TO PATIENT ON EXAMINING TABLE: "Trust me, Senator. Many people have active and fulfilling sex lives long after they've retired from Congress."

 Danny Shanahan
Present Day Cartoonist in the *New Yorker*

I've never taken up with a congressman in my life.... I've never gone below the Senate.

 Barbara Howar
(1934–) Writer, Actress

Are we going to deny ourselves our best politicians because of their sex lives?

 Barbara Streisand
(1942–) Singer, Actress, Director

Well, Teddy, I see you've changed your position on offshore drilling.

 Howell Heflin
(1921–) Senator; on seeing a photo of Ted Kennedy in a compromising position with a woman in a boat

OUR CULTURE

Insightful Observations on
PRESIDENTIAL SEX

It's a mess ain't it? He's a horny little toad.

Dolly Parton
(1946–) Singer, Songwriter,
Actress; **on Bill Clinton**

I would rather have a president who does it to a woman than a president who does it to his country.

Shirley MacLaine
(1934–) Actress, Dancer,
Writer

Leaders of countries called me and asked for sex. You look at any picture of a politician with some girls around him and at least three of them will be mine.... If I really came out and talked, I could have stopped NAFTA.

Heidi Fleiss
(1965–) Hollywood Madame

If a man is running the country great and going out at night dressed as a woman, is it really our business?

Paul Reiser
(1957–) Actor, Writer,
Comedian

The only reason I'm not running for president is I'm afraid no woman would come forth and say she's slept with me.

Garry Shandling
(1949–) Actor, Writer,
Comedian

THE GUIDE TO LAUGHING AT SEX

OUR CULTURE

Insightful Observations on ROYAL SEX

Oh God. I'll just live inside your trousers or something.

😎 **Prince Charles**
(1948–) Prince of England;
in a phone conversation with Camilla Parker Bowles

Henry was eighteen when we met and I was Queen of France. He came down from north to Paris with a mind like Aristotle's and a form like mortal sin. We shattered the Commandments on the spot.

😎 **Katherine Hepburn**
in *The Lion in Winter* (1968)
written James Goldman

Oh stop, I want to feel my way along you, all over you and up and down you.

😎 **Prince Charles**
(1948–) to Camilla Parker
Bowles (1947-)

JOHN MALKOVICH: The countess has promised me extensive use of her gardens. It seems her husband's fingers are not as green as they once were.
GLENN CLOSE: Maybe not, but from what I hear, all his friends are gardeners.

🙂 *Dangerous Liasons*
(1988)

😎 = IDEALIST   🙂 = REALIST   😊 = CYNIC

231

OUR CULTURE

Insightful Observations on
FAME & SEX

You can be ugly as I am and still get laid more than the best-looking guy. Because I'm in KISS.

Gene Simmons
(1949–) Rock Star; KISS

Any idiot can get laid when they're famous. That's easy. It's getting laid when you're not famous that takes some talent.

Kevin Bacon
(1958–) Actor

Being a sixty-four-year-old sex symbol is a hell of a weight to carry.

John Forsythe
(1918–) Actor; **on fame later in life**

Michael Jackson is the polar opposite of President Clinton in many respects. Michael Jackson is constantly, constantly, desperately trying to make us believe he's having sex with women.

David Letterman
(1947–) Humorist, Talk Show Host

I have found that it [fame] doesn't get you laid and you don't get as much free stuff as you'd think.

Anthony Edwards
(1962–) Actor

232

OUR CULTURE

Insightful Observations on VIRTUE & SEX

For some people, sex is so good it's scary. Is that bad? Let's be reasonable: if sex is good, lots of sex is even better. Good sex can make you a better person. So lots of sex might make you the finest person you can be. Your body isn't just your temple, it's also your holy brothel.

Eurydice
Present Day Sex Columnist
For *Spin and Gear*

A slut shares his sexuality the way a philanthropist shares her money—because they have a lot of it to share, because it makes them happy to share it, because sharing makes the world a better place.

**Dossie Easton &
Catherine A. Liszt**
Therapist, Writer & Writer,
Educator

I feel that the older I get, the more shameless I feel. And in a sense, more pure.

Maria Irene Fornes
(1930–) Playwright

OUR CULTURE

Insightful Observations on
TRADITION & SEX

The first day of Spring was once the time for taking the young virgins into the fields, there in dalliance to set an example in fertility for nature to follow. Now we just set the clock an hour ahead and change the oil in the crankcase.

E.B. White
(1899–1985) Writer

We've surrounded the most vital and commonplace human function with a vast morass of taboos, conventions, hypocrisy, and plain claptrap.

Ilka Chase
(1905–1978) Actress, Writer

234

THE GUIDE TO LAUGHING AT SEX

INTERNATIONAL SEX

Insightful Observations on
SEX AROUND THE WORLD

In various stages of her life, a woman resembles the continents of the world. From 13 to 18, she's like Africa—virgin territory, unexplored; from 18 to 30 she's like Asia—hot and exotic; from 30 to 45, she's like America, fully explored and free with her resources; from 45 to 55, she's like Europe, fully explored and exhausted, but not without places of interest; after 55, she's like Australia—everybody knows it's down there but nobody much cares.

 Al Boliska
Humorist

In Lebanon men are allowed to have sex with female animals. Having sex with a male animal is punishable by death.

Sex, A Users Guide
by Stephen Arnott

In 1993 a Japanese mail-order service was started allowing the customers to buy the used panties of school girls, housewives, nurses and widows.

Sex, A Users Guide
by Stephen Arnott

Sex in France is a comedy; in England it is a tragedy; in America it's a melodrama; in Italy it's an opera; in Germany, a reason to take up philosophy.

Author Unknown

INSIGHTFUL OBSERVATIONS TO SHARE

INTERNATIONAL SEX

Insightful Observations on AMERICAN SEX

Americans, unlike many other nationalities, have never accepted the idea that a man should have a wife to bear his children and a mistress to provide romance. Even in the relatively new concept of couples living together without marriage, the emphasis has been on mutual emotional support. Americans want love to work. They are more committed to the ideal than any other people in history.

Ann Landers
(1918–2002) Advice Columnist

This country is into tits and ass.

Neil Simon
(1927–) Playwright

In expressing love, we belong among the undeveloped countries.

Saul Bellow
(1915–) Canadian Writer

The great American formula for sex is: a kiss on the lips, a hand on the breast, and a dive for the groin.

William H. Masters
(1915–2001) Biologist, Sexual Therapist

The mammary fixation is the most infantile and most American of the sex fetishes.

Molly Haskell
(1939–) Writer, Film Critic

You know how Americans are— when it comes to sex, the men can't keep from lying and the women can't keep from telling the truth.

Robin Zander
(1953–) Musician

In America sex is an obsession, in other parts of the world it is a fact.

Marlene Dietrich
(1901–1992) German Actress

236

INTERNATIONAL SEX

Insightful Observations on
ENGLISH SEX

It's only human nature after all,
For a boy to get a girl against a wall,
And slip his abomination into her accommodation,
To increase the population of the coming generation.

 English Folk Rhyme

It is impossible to obtain a conviction for sodomy from an English jury. Half of them don't believe it can be physically done, and the other half are doing it.

 Winston Churchill
(1874–1965) British
Statesman

It has to be admitted that we English have sex on the brain, which is a very unsatisfactory place to have it.

 Malcolm Muggeridge
(1903–1990) Journalist, Sage

Like every young man grown up in England, he was conditioned to get a hard-on in the presence of certain fetishes, and then conditioned to feel shame about his new reflexes.

 Thomas Pynchon
(1937–) Novelist

This sort of thing may be tolerated by the French—but we are British, thank God.

 Viscount Montgomery
(1887–1976) British Field
Marshal; **on homosexuality**

237

INTERNATIONAL SEX

Insightful Observations on EUROPEAN SEX

Bed, as the Italian proverb succinctly puts it, is the poor man's opera.

Aldous Huxley
(1894–1963) Author

In Spain, lust is in the air. There is nothing clandestine about the Spanish appreciation of sex, nothing inhibited or restrained. That is why there are very few sexual crimes in Spain.

Fernando Diaz-Plaja
Writer

France is the only place where you can make love in the afternoon without people hammering on your door.

Barbara Cartland
(1901–2000) British
Romance Novelist

It's true that the French have a certain obsession with sex, but it's a particularly adult obsession. France is the thriftiest of all nations; to a Frenchman, sex provides the most economical way to have fun.

Anita Loos
(1888–1981) Author;
ScreenWriter

German men always do things by the numbers. They seem to base their amorous advances on pages from a strange and misplaced book, a book that will never make the best-seller charts here in America. They try to give you the impression that to accompany them from the airplane and share their bed would be a contribution toward some better, super-world.

Trudy Baker & Rachel Jones
Authors; *Coffee Tea or Me*

238

REGULATING SEX

Insightful Observations on REGULATED SEX

The puritans should wear fig leaves on their eyes.

 Stanislaw J. Lec
(1909–1966) Writer

If adultery were made a federal crime punishable by fine, the national debt would be wiped out in a year or two.

 Eunice Zoghlin Edgar
Director, Wisconsin ACLU

What is liberty if you can't control your own bedroom?

 Particia R. Schroeder
1940–) U.S. Congresswoman

Nothing makes religious people as nervous as sex, or at least unregulated sex.

 Eric Berne
(1910–1970) Psychoanalyst

When authorities warn of the sinfulness of sex, there is an important lesson to be learned: do not have sex with the authorities.

 Matt Groening
(1954–) Writer, Humorist, Cartoonist

Why should we take advice on sex from the Pope? If he knows anything about it, he shouldn't.

 George Bernard Shaw
(1856–1950) Playwright, Novelist, Critic

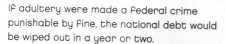 = IDEALIST   = REALIST   😀 = CYNIC

GETTING STARTED

AVOIDING SEX

EXPERIENCING SEX

EXPERIMENTING

COMMON PROBLEMS

SEX AND SOCIETY

REGULATING SEX

Insightful Observations on
SEX AND THE LAW

I regret to say that we are powerless to act in cases of oral-genital intimacy, unless it has obstructed interstate commerce.

J. Edgar Hoover
(1895–1972) Former Director of the FBI

What he does on his own time is up to him.

Harlon Copeland
County Sheriff; **about a deputy caught exposing himself in public**

I like to use the term manipulation of the genitalia.

Bill Stookey
Police Spokesman; **on what Pee-wee Herman was caught doing in an adult theater**

Women are like banks, boy. Breaking and entering is a serious business.

Joe Orton
(1933–1967) Playwright, Actor

The majority of states which have reviewed this issue agree [laws concerning indecent exposure] include only genitalia.

Julie Lewis
Public Defender; **arguing before the North Carolina Supreme Court on the legality of "mooning"**

Lust is an appetite that needs to be regulated.

William F. Buckley Jr.
(1925–) Political Columnist, Author

THE GUIDE TO LAUGHING AT SEX

REGULATING SEX

Insightful Observations on SEX ON TV

I've got an idea. Let's fill the whole screen with tits.

😆 **Hunt Stromberg**
(1894–1968) Producer, Writer, Director; **about a documentary on the South Seas**

On TV you can use sex to sell anything except sex.

😊 **Stephanie Black**
Head of Marketing, Playboy Channel

Sex on television can't hurt you unless you fall off.

😊 **Author Unknown**

Corporately, we believe in orgasms.

😊 **Warren Littlefield**
(1952–) Television Executive

The cable TV sex channels don't expand our horizons, don't make us better people and don't come in clearly enough.

😊 **Bill Maher**
(1956–) Writer, TV Talk Show Host

REGULATING SEX

Insightful Observations on
SEX IN THE MOVIES

A movie without sex would be like a candy bar without nuts.

Earl Wilson
(1907–1987) Columnist

There is nothing unnatural about kissing. If more husbands would learn from the stages and pictures just how to kiss, and then go home and practice on their wives, there would be happier homes and fewer divorces.

Fiorello H. La Guardia
(1882–1947) Former Mayor of New York City, Congressman; **on the 1926 federal censorship of movies which showed 'too much kissing'**

So this is the Year of the Woman? Well, yes, this has been a very good year for women. Demi Moore was sold to Robert Redford for a million. Uma Thurman went for $40,000 to Mr. De Niro. While just three years ago Richard Gere bought Julia Roberts for ... what was it? $3,000? I'd say that was real progress.

Michelle Pfeiffer
(1957–) Actress

Let's have sex.

The meaning of "Titanic" in Arabic slang

THE GUIDE TO LAUGHING AT SEX

REGULATING SEX

Insightful Observations on
MOVIE RATINGS

"G" means the hero gets the girl. "R" means the villain gets the girl. And "X" means everybody gets the girl.

 Kirk Douglas
(1916–) Actor

Scenes of passion ... should not be introduced when not essential to the plot.... In general, the passion should be so treated that these scenes do not stimulate the lower and baser elements.

 Motion Picture Producers and Distributors of America
Code of March 31, 1930

If a man is pictured chopping off a woman's breast, it only gets an R rating; but if, God forbid, a man is pictured kissing a woman's breast, it gets an X rating. Why is violence more acceptable than tenderness?

Sally Struthers
(1948–) Actress

Our American people are a pretty homely and wholesome crowd. Cockeyed philosophies of life, ugly sex situations, cheap jokes and dirty dialogue are not wanted. Decent people don't like this sort of stuff and it's our job to see to it that they get none of it.

 Joseph Breen
Code of Enforcement Officer for the Motion Picture Association of America

Won't the new "Suggested for mature audiences" protect out youngsters from such films? I don't believe so. I know many forty-five-year-old men with the mentality of six-year-olds, and my feeling is that they should not see pictures either.

Shirley Temple Black
(1928–) Movie Actress, Diplomat

REGULATING SEX

Insightful Observations on CENSORSHIP

Murder is a crime. Writing about it isn't. Sex is not a crime, but writing about it is. Why?

Larry Flynt
(1942–) *Hustler* Publisher;
Civil Liberties Advocate

Censorship is the strongest drive in human nature—sex is only a weak second.

Phil Kerby
Writer

I've got nothing against sex, it's a marvelous human activity, but it was watching others do it all the time that got me down.

John Trevelyan
British Film Censor; **on why he resigned**

Every obscene, lewd, or lascivious act, and every filthy book, pamphlet, picture, paper, letter, writing, print or other publication of an indecent character ... is hereby declared to be nonmalleable matter.

U.S. Criminal Code
March 4, 1909

THE GUIDE TO LAUGHING AT SEX

REGULATING SEX

Insightful Observations on
SECRECY & SEX

I had to lie so much about sex, first when I was fifteen, because I wasn't supposed to be having it. And then when I got older, I lied to everybody I was having sex with so I could have sex with other people.

Cybill Shepherd
(1950–) Actress

Traditionally, sex has been a very private, secretive activity. Herein perhaps lies its powerful force for uniting people in a strong bond. As we make sex less secretive, we may rob it of its power to hold men and women together.

Thomas Szasz
(1920–) Psychiatrist

What people do behind closed doors is certainly not my concern unless I'm behind there with them.

Dolly Parton
(1946–) Singer, Songwriter, Actress

If sex is so personal, why are we expected to share it with someone else?

Lily Tomlin
(1939–) Comedian, Actress

REGULATING SEX

Insightful Observations on
MENTAL ILLNESS & SEX

SEXUAL ACTIVITIES ONCE CONSIDERED MENTAL ILLNESSES:

1. Exhibitionism – The desire to display one's genitalia to the world was once considered a mental illness.
2. Sexual Sadism – Those who derived sexual pleasure from inflicting pain upon their sexual partners was thought to be mentally ill with criminal leanings.
3. Sexual Masochism – The desire to be hurt in some manner during sex (beaten, whipped, spanked). Women who were masochistic were thought to suffer from hysteria.
4. Masturbation – The act has historically been linked to several mental illnesses and possibly the devil.
5. Voyeurism – The act of observing strangers naked or having sex has been seen as a sign of a mental illness.
6. Cross-dressing – Cross-dressers of the late 1800s were put with the criminally insane.
7. Homosexuality – At various stages of history, homosexuality was linked to mental illness and criminal activity ... at other times it was thought that you could "deprogram" homosexuals. In 1973, the American Psychiatric Association dropped homosexuality from its list of mental disorders.

The Sex Lovers Book of Lists
by Ron Louis and David Copeland

THE GUIDE TO LAUGHING AT SEX

REGULATING SEX

Insightful Observations on
SIN & SEX

Christ dies for our sins. Dare we make his martyrdom meaningless by not committing them?

😇 **Jules Feiffer**
(1929–) Cartoonist, Playwright

Contempt of sexuality is a crime against life.

😇 **Friedrich Nietzsche**
(1844–1900) German Philosopher

Mother, you who conceived without sinning, teach me how to sin without conceiving.

😇 **Author Unknown**

Should we all confess our sins to one another, we would all laugh at one another of our lack of originality.

😉 **Kahlil Gibran**
(1883–1931) Philospher

Fashions in sin change.

😉 **Lillian Hellman**
(1905–1984) Playwright, Novelist

The Anglo-Saxon conscience does not prevent the Anglo-Saxon from sinning, it merely prevents him from enjoying his sin.

🙂 **Salvador de Madariaga**
(1886–1978) Writer, Scholar, Diplomat

😇 = IDEALIST   😉 = REALIST   🙂 = CYNIC

GETTING STARTED

AVOIDING SEX

EXPERIENCING SEX

EXPERIMENTING

COMMON PROBLEMS

SEX AND SOCIETY

REGULATING SEX

Insightful Observations on
RELIGION & SEX

God and I have a great relationship but we both see other people.

 Dolly Parton
(1946–) Singer, Songwriter, Actress

Religion is probably, after sex, the second oldest resource which human beings have available to them for blowing their minds.

 Susan Sontag
(1933-) Author, Director

All religions have problems with sex. Sex is at the heart of people's identity and God is the symbol for ultimate meaning. These things are always intertwined.

 John Spong
(1931–) Episcopalian Bishop

I don't know whether you've ever had a woman eat an apple while you're doing it.... Well, you can imagine how it affects you.

 Henry Miller
(1891–1980) Novelist

Sex has become the religion of the most civilized portions of the earth. The orgasm has replaced the Cross as the focus of longing and the image of fulfillment.

 Malcolm Muggeridge
(1903–1990) Journalist, Sage

Sex is God's joke on human beings.

 Bette Davis
(1908–1989) Actress

THE GUIDE TO LAUGHING AT SEX

REGULATING SEX

Insightful Observations on
CATHOLICISM & SEX

Nuns are sexy.

Madonna
(1958–) Singer, Songwriter, Actress

If you're only going to have ten rules, I don't know if adultery should be one of them.

Ted Turner
(1938–) Entrepreneur; **on revising the Ten Commandments**

Life in Lubbock, Texas taught me two things. One is that God loves you and you're going to burn in hell. The other is that sex is the most awful, filthy thing on earth. And you should save it for someone you love.

Butch Hancock
(1945–) Singer, Songwriter

Christianity has done love a great service by making it a sin.

Anatole France
(1844–1924) Writer

Have you swallowed your husband's semen in the hope that because of your diabolical deed he might burn all the more with love and desire for you? If you have done this, you should do penance for seven years on legitimate holy days.

Burchard of Worms
(950–1025) German Bishop

To hear many religious people talk, one would think God created the torso, head, legs and arms, but the Devil slapped on the genitals.

Don Schrader
Model, Writer

LEARNING ABOUT SEX

Insightful Observations on
BIRDS AND THE BEES

 Author Unknown

While I was visiting friends, the youngest member of the family, a seven-year-old boy, began to question his mother insistently about the facts of life. Patiently, she explained the miracle of life from conception, when large numbers of sperm raced towards the as yet unfertilized egg, through the nine months of pregnancy, to birth. As the lad sat quietly pondering over what he had heard, his expression changed gradually from puzzlement to understanding. Suddenly he grinned from ear to ear, leapt up, threw his arms around his mother, and cried, "And I won the race!"

ONE SMALL GIRL TO ANOTHER AS THEY SIT READING NEWSPAPER: "I think oral sex is when they only just talk about it."

 Robert Weber
Present Day Cartoonist in the *New Yorker*

FATHER TALKING TO HIS SON: You'd better ask your grandparents about that, son—my generation is very uncomfortable talking about abstinence.

 Robert Mankoff
Present Day Cartoonist in the *New Yorker*

I was very sheltered growing up. I knew nothing about sex. My mother said this: "Sex is a dirty, disgusting thing you save for somebody you love.

 Carol Henry
Writer

250

LEARNING ABOUT SEX

Insightful Observations on SEX EDUCATION

The best sex education for kids is when Daddy pats Mommy on the fanny when he comes home from work.

Dr. William H. Masters
(1915–2001) Biologist, Sexual Therapist; Masters & Johnson Institute

Let's teach a ... follow-up class to sex education. Call it Reality 101—hammering home to a sixteen-year-old teen that he or she is going to have to quit school, quit video games, quit hanging out, and work a fifty-hour week dumping frozen chicken tenders into hot oil just so you can keep little Scooter Junior in Similac. Trust me, that's a bigger deterrent to teenage sex than the backseat of a Yugo.

Dennis Miller
(1953–) Actor, Comedian

If sex is such a natural phenomenon, how come there are so many books on how to?

Bette Midler
(1944–) Actress, Singer, Comedian

From bestsellers to comic books, any child who hasn't acquired an extensive sex education by the age of twelve belongs in remedial reading.

Will Stanton
(1918–) Writer

I didn't know how babies were made until I was pregnant with my fourth child five years later.

Loretta Lynn
(1935–) Country Singer, Songwriter

INSIGHTFUL OBSERVATIONS TO SHARE

251

LEARNING ABOUT SEX

Insightful Observations on
SEX ED IN SCHOOL

If you bring a plastic penis into the classroom as they do in Sweden, that removes all the mystery.

 Jane Fonda
(1937–) Actress

We teach teenagers what to do in the front seat of cars, and now we should teach them what to do in the back seats.

 Joycelyn Elders
(1933–) U.S. Surgeon General

I am against sex ed in the schools, because sex is so much more fun when it's dirty and sinful.

 Florence King
(1936–) Author

Had America has become a country where a classroom discussion of the Ten Commandments is impermissible, but teacher instructions in safe sodomy are to be mandatory?

 Pat Buchanan
(1938–) Writer, Political Columnist

I don't worry too much about sex education in the schools. If the kids learn it like they do everything else, they won't know how.

 Milton Berle
(1908–2002) Comedian, Actor

THE GUIDE TO LAUGHING AT SEX

LEARNING ABOUT SEX

Insightful Observations on SELLING WITH SEX

The adman has discovered the vagina and it's like the next thing going. What happened is that the adman ran out of parts of the body. So the adman sat back and said, What's left? And some smart guy said, The Vagina!

 David Ogilvy
(1911–1999) Advertising Executive

Sex! What is that but [life], after all? We're all of us selling sex because we're all selling life.

 Alvin Chereskin
Advertising Executive

Sometimes the photographers would pose me in a low-necked nightgown and tell me to bend down and pick up the pails. They were not shooting the pails.

 Jane Russell
(1921–) Actress

Being accused of making money by selling sex in Hollywood, home of the casting couch and the gratuitous nude scene, is so rich with irony that it's a better subject for a comic novel than a column ... they're charging Heidi Fleiss with pandering in a town in which the verb is an art form.

 Anna Quindlen
(1952–) Author, Journalist

Society drives people crazy with lust and calls it advertising.

 John Lahr
(1941–) Writer, Critic

Our culture uses sex in the most cynical way to "sell" anything—even though we blanch when sex is presented simply, or sold for itself.

 Susie Bright
(1958–) Writer, Editor

LEARNING ABOUT SEX

Insightful Observations on
FEMALE SEX SYMBOLS

And here they are, Jayne Mansfield.

 Jack Parr
(1918–) TV Talk Show Host;
introducing Ms. Mansfield

I have never quite understood this sex symbol business but if I'm going to be a symbol of something, I'd rather have it be sex than some of the other things they've got symbols for.

Being a sex symbol has to do with attitude, not looks. Most men think it's looks, most women know otherwise.

Marilyn Monroe
(1926–1962) Actress

Kathleen Turner
(1954–) Actress

There is no sign that her acting would ever have progressed beyond the scope of the restless shoulders and the protuberant breasts; her body technique was the gangster's technique—she toted a breast like a man totes a gun.

 Graham Greene
(1904–1991) Writer; on
Actress Jean Harlow

A plumber's idea of Cleopatra.

W.C. Fields
(1879–1946) Actor,
Screenwriter; **referring to
Mae West**

Think of me as a sex symbol for the men who don't give a damn.

 Phyllis Diller
(1917–) Comedian, Actress,
Author

254

LEARNING ABOUT SEX

Insightful Observations on
MALE SEX SYMBOLS

If I had as many love affairs as you have given me credit for, I would now be speaking to you from a jar in the Harvard Medical School.

   Frank Sinatra
(1915–1998) Singer, Actor; **at a press conference**

If I've still got my pants on in the second scene, I think they've sent me the wrong script.

   Mel Gibson
(1956–) Actor, Director, Producer

I'm a sex machine to both genders. It's all very exhausting. I need a lot of sleep.

   Rupert Everett
(1959–) Actor

The homosexual community wants me to be gay. The heterosexual community wants me to be straight. Every [writer] thinks, "I'm the journalist who's going to make him talk." I pray for them. I pray that they get a life and stop living mine!

   Ricky Martin
(1971–) Singer

Once they call you a Latin lover, you're in real trouble. Women expect an Oscar performance in bed.

   Marcello Mastroianni
(1924–1996) Actor

If you become a star, you don't change, everyone else does.

   Kirk Douglas
(1916–) Actor

 = IDEALIST   = REALIST   😊 = CYNIC

SEX AND SOCIETY

255

LEARNING ABOUT SEX

Insightful Observations on
DEFINING PORNOGRAPHY

Pornography is literature designed to be read with one hand.

Angela Lambert
Author

The difference between pornography and erotica is the lighting.

Gloria Leonard
(1940–) Porn Star, Publisher

If we define pornography as any message from any commercial medium that is intended to arouse sexual excitement, then it is clear that most advertisements are covertly pornographic.

Philip Stater
Sociologist

Obscenity is whatever gives a judge an erection.

Author Unknown

THE GUIDE TO LAUGHING AT SEX

LEARNING ABOUT SEX

Insightful Observations on DISCOVERING PORNOGRAPHY

Everybody got it wrong. I said I was into porn again, not born again.

I heard there was a lot of porno stuff on the Web. I looked for it and couldn't find it. Then I found this one site and it was twenty bucks a month! Twenty bucks a month! Hustler's only $3.99.

On the 100th anniversary of the National Geographic, I recalled how as a kid I used to look at that magazine for photographs of topless natives. It was permissible to show such nakedness because these were women of color. Of course, this was before Playboy, Penthouse, and Hustler; but even these men's magazines have an unspoken agreement never to show nipples on the cover, no matter how gynecological they get on the inside pages, where sweaty ladies appear to be searching in vain for lost objects.

Okay, if you want to get down and to the nitty-gritty.... Let's say I'm watching a porno, for instance—and I've analyzed it, to see what makes me tick—I do like to see two women together. It turns me on more than anything else. That's what rings my chimes.

 Billy Idol
(1955–) Singer, Punk Rocker

 Ben Affleck
(1972–) Actor, Writer

Paul Krassner
(1932–) Actor, Comedian

 Tom Jones
(1940–) Singer

LEARNING ABOUT SEX

Insightful Observations on
REACTIONS TO PORNOGRAPHY

To men, porno movies are beautiful love stories with all the boring stuff taken out.

Richard Jeni
Comedian, Actor, Writer

I think porn is fine. I like to watch people fuck.

David Duchovny
(1960–) Actor

If anyone is exploited by Penthouse, it's men. Women are paid handsomely to appear in the magazine, while men have to pay for the privilege of seeing them.

Kathy Keeton Guccione
(1939–) Stripper turned Publishing Executive

If he has done nothing else for American culture, he has given it two of the great lies of the twentieth century: I buy it for the fiction and I buy it for the interview.

Nora Ephron
(1941–) Writer, Director; on Hugh Hefner and *Playboy*

My reactions to porno films are as follows: After the first ten minutes, I want to go home and screw. After the first twenty minutes, I never want to screw again as long as I live.

Erica Jong
(1942–) Writer, Poet

I happen to like old-school porn because I like the natural body. The women in this new porn, their boobs are just so weird and high and far out, they look like those goldfish with the puffy eyes.

Margaret Cho
(1968–) Comedian, Actress

258

Insightful Observations

_____

_____

_____

_____

_____

_____

_____

_____

_____

_____

_____

_____

_____

_____

_____

_____

_____

INSIGHTFUL OBSERVATIONS TO SHARE

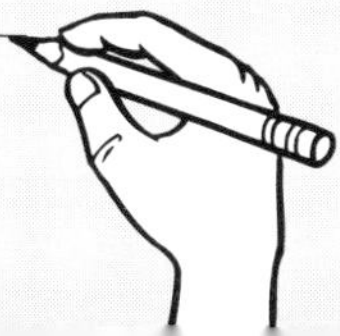

Guide to Laughing Institute Honorees

The GTL institute recognizes those listed below for their
wit and wisdom, for helping others to laugh and learn about SEX,
and for the impact they have had on our culture.

(GTL Institute members are encouraged to further explore the works of those honored herein)

Laughing at Sex Hall of Fame

Woody Allen
(1935–)
Director, Actor, Writer

Helen Gurley Brown
(1922–)
Author, Editor

Dr. Alex Comfort
(1920–2000)
British Writer, Sexologist

Quentin Crisp
(1908–1999)
Writer

Rodney Dangerfield
(1921–)
Actor, Comedian

Phyllis Diller
(1917–)
Comedian, Actress, Author

Nora Ephron
(1941–)
Writer, Director

Germaine Greer
(1939–)
Feminist, Writer, Lecturer

Xaviera Hollander
(1943–)
Madam, Writer

Erica Jong
(1942–)
Writer, Poet

Ann Landers
(1918–2002) Advice Columnist

Madonna
(1958–)
Singer, SongWriter, Actress

Robert Mankoff
Present Day
Cartoonist, the *New Yorker*

Paul Mazursky
(1930–)
Actor, Director, Writer

The *New Yorker*

P.J. O'Rourke
(1947–)
Humorist, Journalist

Dorothy Parker
(1893–1967)
Writer

Joan Rivers
(1933–)
Actress, Comedian

Sex A Users Guide

Writers of HBO's
Sex and the City

William Shakespeare
(1564–1616)
Playwright, Poet

Garry Shandling
(1949–)
Actor, Writer, Comedian

Mark Twain
(1835–1910)
Writer, Humorist

Gore Vidal
(1925–)
Novelist, Playwright, Essayist

Mae West
(1892–1980)
Actress, Writer

THE GUIDE TO LAUGHING AT SEX

Register membership and contribute "Insightful Observations" at

Guide to Laughing Institute Honorees

THE GUIDE TO LAUGHING AT SEX

Register membership and contribute "Insightful Observations" at
www.GuideToLaughing.com
263

Guide to Laughing Institute Honorees

THE GUIDE TO LAUGHING AT SEX

Register membership and contribute "Insightful Observations" at

www.GuideToLaughing.com

Guide to Laughing Institute Influencers

The following individuals are recognized for their influence and example in shaping the *Guide to Laughing* handbooks, and for their contribution in helping others to laugh and learn about life.

Abby Goldstein
Adam Pergament
Adam Shankman
Adam Goldenberg
Adeo Ressi
Alan Wolpert
Alex Dube
Alex Garbuio
Alex Lightman
Alisa Barry
Allen Tuller
Allesandro Tecchini
Amos Newman
Amy Einhorn
Amy Eisenberg
Amy Karl
Amy Neunsinger
Amy Van Dyke
Andrew Schupak
Andriana Meyer
Andy Panzo
Angie Schwor
ANKA
Ann Johnstad
Ann Magnuson
Anna Gatterdam
Anne Neunsinger
Anthony Haden-Guest
April Uchitel
Arnie Gullov-Singh
Ashley Fox
Barbara Blechman
Barbara Saunders
Becky Hamilton
Berkley Hanes
Betty Wasserman
Bianca Harzbecker
Bill Dolan
Bill Goins
Bill Nelson
Bob Epstein
Bobette Cohn
Bonnie Solomon
Brad Greenspan
Brad Beckerman
Brad Nye
Brett Brewer
Brett Wright
Brian Seth Hurst
Bridget Sorenson
Brigitte Bourdeau
Brooke Carey

Brooks Martin
Bruce Fischer
Bruce Talan
Carl Bressler
Carlo McCormick
Caroline Applegate
Caroline Sommers
Carter Pottash
Cathy Barsky
Catrina Gregory
Caz Dawkins
Charles Bush
Charles Sommer
Charles Goldschein
Charles Fedak
Chris Biller
Chris Dewolfe
Chris Lipp
Chris McCall
Chris Soumas
Chris Theberge
Chris Hensley
Christine Kozler
Christine Masterson
Chuck Fedak
Claire LaBraun
Clare Kleinedler
Colin Sowa
Corey Reynolds
Corey Scholibo
Courtney Nichols
Craig Filipacchi
Cynthia Cohen
Dan Bassett
Dan Pelson
Dan Loeb
Dana Albarella
Dancenoise
Darren Romanelli
Darrin Higman
Dave Scarpa
Dave Welker
Davia Smith
David Bennahaum
David Hershkovitz
David Hyman
David Freeman
David Harliston
David Spade
David Wilk
Dean Factor
Deanna McDaniel

Debbie Levine
Debbie Vitalie
Deigo Uchitel
Desiree Gruber
Dominic Ianno
Don Gatterdam
Don Ressler
Donald Graham
Donni Briar
Donnie Osmond
Doug Rushkoff
Elise Newman
EMILY
Eric Bogosian
Eric Troop
Eric B
Eric Barnes
Erin Cartwright
Evan Forster
FLO
Frank Keating
Frederic Bien
Gabriel Snyder
Garnie Nygren
Gary Dwardin
Gayle Shea
Genevive Moore
George Brandle
George Brightman
George Goldstein
George Racz
Gerry McIntyre
Gigi Stone
GILES
Glenn Meyers
GLORIA
Gordon Gould
Greg Cass
Greg Clayman
Harry Magnie
Harvey Isaacs
Hedi Kim
Helen Roche
Henry Eshelman
Henry Shea
Henry E. Scott
Holly Schwarz
Howard Stern
Ian Shapolsky
Ian Tong
Irwin Gold
Isadora Gullov-Singh

Jack Black
Jack Ohringer
Jacqui Samuels
Jade Li Kim
James Healy
Jamie Levy
Jane Hamilton
Jane Mount
Janice Gates
Jason Calacanis
Jason Oates
Jay Goodman
Jay Rodriguez
Jay Tralese
JD Heilpren
Jeff Burke
Jeff Dachis
Jeff Henslin
Jeff Kravitz
Jeff Pollack
Jeff Stern
Jeff Weiss
Jeffery Gomanor
Jen Charat
Jennifer Anderson
Jennifer Enderlin
Jennifer Weis
Jenny Pelson
Jenny Landy
Jeremy Roberts
Jeremy Umland
Jerry Speigel
Jessica Felshman
Jilli Moss
Jim Panozza
Jim Wagner
Jim Wexler
Joan Barnes
Joanna Barnes
Joanna Kim
Joanna Scott
Jodi Rappaport
Joel Gotler
Joel Kades
Joey Arias
Joey Cavella
John Kelly
John F. Kennedy Jr.
John Kjenner
John Lenard
John Mchugh
John Nicholson

John Warrin
Johnie Fodor
Jon Birge
Jon Marc Houmard
Jonathan Anastas
Jordan Crandel
Josette Wys
Josh Harris
Josh Rose
Josh Berman
Joyce Isaacs
JP Theberge
Judith Regan
Julie Halston
Justine Musk
Kaiama Glover
Kara Nygren
Karen Salmonsohn
Karen Stewart
Karen Switlyk
Katherine Leonard
Kelly Rodriques
Kelly Jenkins
Ken Beckerman
Ken Campbell
Ken Rutkowski
Kevin Kelly
Kevin Kent
Kevin Fox
Keiran Culkin
Kiersten Burke
Kim Kurilla
Kim Serafin
Korey Kolessa
Lady Bunny
Lancelot Link
Laura Goldschein
Laura Shanahan
Laurel Wells
Lauren Perle
Leda Voln
Lenore Pavlakos
Leslie Morava
Leslie France
Leslie Wells
Lisa Feldman
Lisa Goldschein
Lisa Goldschein
Lisa Kanino
Lisa Malin
Lisa Baruch
Lisa Gold
Lisa Thompson
Lisa Towel
Liz Heller
Liz Smith
Loleh Zayanderoudi

Lori Ann Vander Pluym
Lynn Maloney
LYPSINKA
Macalister Clabaugh
Mads Kornerup
MARA
Marc Landau
Marc Levey
Marc Scarpa
Marc Shaiman
Marc Von Arx
Marco Ilardi
Margie Gilmore
Marie Nygren
Marisa Bowe
Mark Arrow
Mark Goodman
Mark Muscarella
Mark Tribe
Mark Williams
Marty Fienberg
Matt Coffin
Maurice Bernstein
Max Lodish
Meg Gilllentine
Melinda Farrell
Melissa Blau
Michael Barlow
Michael Dowling
Michael Kantrow
Michael Leapold
Michael Marx
Michael Diament
Michele Sebolt
Michelle Madansky
Mike Maggio
Mike Schwarz
Mike Van Styne
Mike Kantrow
Mike Maggio
Mikkel Bondeson
Mindy Espy
Molly McAlpine
Nancy Levie
Natalie Thomas
Natalie Warady
Natasha Esch
Natasha Tsarkova
Neil Gold
Neil Tiles
Neil Wolfson
Nicholas Butterworth
Oduardo Lopez-Yanes
Owen Davis
Owen Masterson
Pam Leapold
PASH

Patricia Medved
Patrick Staves
Patti McConnel
Paul Lance
Paula Heap
Paula Willaims
Paula Kowalczyk
Perry Hagopian
Peter Cohn
Peter Flannigan
Peter Giblin
Peter Jennings
Peter Lavinger
Peter Workman
Phyliss Rosenthal
Pierre Kerangal
PJ Endress
POPPIE
Quinn Nygren
Rabecca Lapinsky
Randi Steinback
Randy Horton
Raven O
Ray Khachatorian
Reed Davis
RICC
Rich Hull
Richard Laermer
Richard Titus
Rob Fenter
Rob Fried
Rob Magnotta
Robert Blechman
Robert Gold
Robert Patterson
Robin Lesser
Rowena Surloff
Ryan Scott
Ryan Spencer
Sabastion Bernardo
Sam Humphries
Sandra Barker
Sarah Manges
Sarah Dumke
Sarah Oscar
Scott Goldschein
Scott Mertz
Scott Wittman
Scott Babrour
Scott Heiferman
Sean Penn
Seth Goldstein
Shahyar Zayanderoudi
Shawn Thompson
Sherry Hilber
Shery Vine
SHERYL

Simon Assaad
Smith Hanes
Spalding Gray
Spence Bovee
Spencer Tunick
Stacy Burka
Stan Topol
Stefan Langan
STEFAN
Stephen Baumer
Steve Macon
Steve Berman
Steve Bilich
Steve Friedman
Steve Nygren
Steve Sackman
Steven Michaud
Stryker Lampe
Stuart Levy
Sunmin Park
Susan Cappa
Susan Swan
Sven Krong
Swan Paik
Tamara Davodavich
Ted Cohen
Ted Werth
Teddy Fiarillo
Tereza Predescu
Tim Giancarlo
Tim Ranson
Tim Hailand
Tim Rosta
Tina Goldschein
Tom Ackerman
Tom Curtin
Tom Rusch
Tom Silverman
Tom Terpin
Tony Drockton
Tony Greenberg
Tonya Corrin
Torrie Dorrell
Trip Dubios
Uncle Burt
VERONICA
Vicki Samuels
Victor Harwood
Warren Zenna
Wayne Harburn
Will Guilliams
William Coplin
Willie Mack
Wylie Stecklow
Xeni Jardin
Yolande Yorke
Zach Leary

Register membership and contribute "Insightful Observations" at

www.GuideToLaughing.com

267

Member Registry

After making a "laughter connection" with someone, the owner of this book is authorized to register that person as a *Guide to Laughing Institute* member. This page serves as record of the date a laughter connection was made and a new member was inducted into the *Guide to Laughing Institute*.

How to register a new member:

1. Have new member agree to obligations on page 9 and choose a member title below
2. Record new member's name, signature, and date of laughter connection
3. Initialize this transaction
4. Welcome new member to the GTL Institute with a firm handshake and warm smile while maintaining eye contact
5. Inform all newly inducted members of their entitlement to all member privileges (See page 1)
6. For updates and information, register contact information at: GTLinstitute.com

Member titles

Apostle of Humility
Emissary of Optimism
Flying Missionary

Goddess
Healing Minister
Mirth Messenger

Urban Shaman
Spiritual Counselor
Prof. of Absolute Reality

TITLE _____

NAME _____

SIGNATURE _____

DATE _____ INITIAL _____

TITLE _____

NAME _____

SIGNATURE _____

DATE _____ INITIAL _____

TITLE _____

NAME _____

SIGNATURE _____

DATE _____ INITIAL _____

TITLE _____

NAME _____

SIGNATURE _____

DATE _____ INITIAL _____

TITLE _____

NAME _____

SIGNATURE _____

DATE _____ INITIAL _____

TITLE _____

NAME _____

SIGNATURE _____

DATE _____ INITIAL _____

TITLE _____

NAME _____

SIGNATURE _____

DATE _____ INITIAL _____

TITLE _____

NAME _____

SIGNATURE _____

DATE _____ INITIAL _____

TITLE _____

NAME _____

SIGNATURE _____

DATE _____ INITIAL _____

TITLE _____

NAME _____

SIGNATURE _____

DATE _____ INITIAL _____

TITLE _____

NAME _____

SIGNATURE _____

DATE _____ INITIAL _____

TITLE _____

NAME _____

SIGNATURE _____

DATE _____ INITIAL _____

TITLE _____

NAME _____

SIGNATURE _____

DATE _____ INITIAL _____

TITLE _____

NAME _____

SIGNATURE _____

DATE _____ INITIAL _____

TITLE _____

NAME _____

SIGNATURE _____

DATE _____ INITIAL _____

TITLE _____

NAME _____

SIGNATURE _____

DATE _____ INITIAL _____

TITLE _____

NAME _____

SIGNATURE _____

DATE _____ INITIAL _____

TITLE _____

NAME _____

SIGNATURE _____

DATE _____ INITIAL _____

Register membership and contribute "Insightful Observations" at

www.GuideToLaughing.com

Founders Note

> *In my search for happiness, the most important discovery I made was that the things worth doing are the things we do for other people: the charming intersection of selfishness and virtue.*
>
> OSCAR HERMAN (1909-1980)   CO-FOUNDER, GTL INSTITUTE

My grandfather, Oscar Herman (1909–1980), a humorist and shoe salesman, inspired the creation of the *Guide to Laughing Institute* by the way he lived. His attitude and our conversations inspired a lifetime search to collect and organize humorous and insightful observations from influential people; and to share these thoughts so others can laugh and learn about life.

The observations in this book have been gathered and edited by GTL Institute members as they find humor and insight in their everyday lives. Each handbook is a compilation of thousands of member experiences including: reading religious texts, novels, reference books, road signs, newspapers, magazines, and instruction manuals; listening to songs on the radio; watching plays, interviews, lectures, movies, TV shows and from everyday conversations and experiences.

Since the formal organization began in 1993, hundreds of people—friends, writers, editors, artists, educators, doctors, executives, and celebrities— have helped shape the Guide to Laughing series.

Thank you for your participation, the *GTL Institute*'s message will continue to grow through the shared wit and laughter of its members.

Shawn Gold
Co-Founder, GTL Institute

Guide to Laughing Institute Founders

Oscar Herman (1909–1980) was an urban Jewish Will Rogers who never met a man he didn't like. He made a living by selling shoes and made a life by sharing his humor. Known as the Mayor of "F" street, a major section of Washington D.C. where he lived, he was revered for having friends of all creeds and colors. A generous champion of the neighborhood children, he often led parades of kids through the drug store candy isle, buying each marcher a treat. Impromptu performances of "Singing in the Rain" or "Alabami Bound," along with hilarious and insightful observations on love, sex, family, and life, were standard fare. Oscar believed the essence of life was connecting with people, and the key to connection was laughter. He was married to his wife Sarah for forty years when he died peacefully in his sleep in 1980. He is missed by the thousands of people whom he touched with his wit and his kindness.

Shawn Gold (1965–) Shawn lives his life with the same spirit and mission as his grandfather Oscar, helping people to laugh and learn about life. Professionally, he has used his understanding of laughter to build a career in helping people to adjust their attitudes. He developed advertising campaigns for some of Americas best known children's brands, wrote relationship advice columns for top women's magazines, and helped to create some of the most popular entertainment sites online. Personally, Shawn is overwhelmed by media and has a short attention span. He is keenly interested in finding the humor in life, thinking about it, and sharing it with others. His goal with *The Guide to Laughing* series is to convey insightful and amusing commentary with the greatest amount of thought per square word. He is married to photographer Amy Neunsinger, who he refers to as "an amazing human," and he is profoundly affected by the experience of being a new dad.

Register membership and contribute "Insightful Observations" at
www.GuideToLaughing.com

To Order Additional Copies

of The Guide to Laughing Institute Member Handbooks:

The Guide to Laughing at LOVE
The Guide to Laughing at SEX

Please visit

www.GuideToLaughing.com

or

Send a Check or Money Order for $12.95
per book (Free Shipping & Handling) to:

Guide to Laughing Orders
c/o Handy Logic Press
8033 Sunset Blvd., #490
Los Angeles, CA 90046

Coming in 2004-2005

The Guide to Laughing at FAMILY
The Guide to Laughing at YOURSELF
The Guide to Laughing at WORK
The Guide to Laughing at HEALTH & AGE
The Guide to Laughing at OUR WORLD
The Guide to Laughing at EATING

And if nothing else, always remember the words of the 21st Century philosopher and singer, Marie Osmond: "If you can look back on something and laugh at it, why not laugh about it now?"

THE GUIDE TO LAUGHING INSTITUTE